Fire Wife

Standing Strong in Your Relationship, Your Life, and Your Dreams

by Tara McIntosh

Cover photo by Brayden McIntosh
Layout by Tom McIntosh
Cover design by Edge of Water Designs, www.edgeofwater.com
Interior formatting by SpicaBookDesign, www.spicabookdesign.com

ISBNs:
Print Book:
978-1-77374-059-1
eBook:
978-1-77374-060-7

Mountain Shadow Publishing
Port Moody, BC
Canada

Preface

My Uncle Ron, the Firefighter

*There's a saying that all men are created equal
but then a few become firefighters.*
JOE BIDEN

My Uncle Ron was one of the finest most respectable men that
I had ever met. He was a professional firefighter married to my
Aunt Chris. It was her first marriage, his second, and boy, did
he ever change our family for the better.

Because of Uncle Ron, I would learn that firefighters are
a social bunch who love to look after people and make them
feel welcome. And just like my beloved uncle, many also know
how to sit back and savor the good things in life, whether that's
cooking, winemaking, or enjoying the great outdoors.

The best memories of my Uncle Ron are of him and my
aunt opening up their hobby farm to host big backyard BBQs for
family and friends. They pulled out all the stops: no half-mea-
sures for them. Ribs on the BBQ? How about an entire roast pig
on a spit, basted for hours instead? From drinking his home-
made red wine to enjoying freshly-caught prawns he'd serve
simply with crackers and cream cheese, Uncle Ron made us all
feel part of a very special kind of family; a family unlike anything
we'd experienced before.

My Uncle Ron was the leader our family really needed. We were in awe of Ron because he embodied all those stately qualities of an admirable chief: he was a strong guy with a quiet strength, a team leader who had a fantastic sense of humor, and someone who had an endless pool of wisdom that we had the pleasure and good fortune to draw from.

When my husband Tom decided to pursue firefighting, Uncle Ron took him under his wing and mentored him. He was fair, he was honorable, and he was a man of the land. And his laugh! Oh my God, it was the best, and can only be described as a person who starts to laugh mid-swig.

Sadly, my Uncle Ron passed away from a very aggressive form of stomach cancer, resulting from years on the job at a time when firefighters didn't have the proper protective gear against the toxic chemicals they are exposed to. He was diagnosed in December and by the following March, he was gone. It was a very real wake-up call to the long-term risks that firefighters like my uncle expose themselves to.

It's hard to lose people who make such an impact on a family; to be honest, ours was never the same without him. Just recently, however, when I visited the same fire hall he once worked at, I came across his picture. It's nice to know he is still all around us. I can still hear his big laugh even now.

My Story

An optimist focuses on the most likely scenario and
a pessimist on the least likely.
ANONYMOUS

I'll be honest: when my husband became a firefighter, I was a reluctant fire wife. For starters, I didn't like his shift work. I also didn't like how much he was away from home, his continuous exhaustion, his new-fangled moods, or the bitterness I felt at having to put my dreams on the shelf for a while. It was fine having an uncle for a firefighter, but being married to one? I'd always loved being independent enough to do my own thing, but now it seemed that every aspect of both our lives would revolve around my husband's career.

Truth be told, I liked my life before firefighting. Prior to my husband becoming a firefighter, he had a good-paying job as part-owner of an awards and recognition shop. He would leave for work at the same time every day and be home in time for dinner every night.

Because his schedule was predictable, I could slip out of the house early in the morning while my family slept to go for a run, a swim, or stop at the gym to stay in shape. It also meant that I could use some evenings to go to lectures, my writing group, or college. Together with being mom to our two sweet boys, my life felt full and well-balanced.

Then something happened.

Seemingly out of left field—and right in the middle of my college aspirations—Tom decided to become a firefighter.

I'm not kidding when I say that my life, as I'd always known it, flashed before my eyes. My husband's new dream meant that he was about to change the trajectory of mine. Everything I'd envisioned for our lives was going to be completely altered, and I was scared as hell. I was also very angry. I knew just how hard fire life could be on a marriage, and I thought he'd lost his mind.

For the next five years, my husband tried to get on as a firefighter with the city. In between, he became a volunteer firefighter with two separate districts. He took night classes to finish getting his college credits and, just to add to the mix, he took a four-month firefighting course at the Justice Institute.

While I admired his fierce perseverance, the reality for me meant that my media and communications degree would have to be put on hold. The disbelief I felt towards what I thought was my husband's early (at age thirty-four) "midlife crisis" was off the charts. Surely, I believed, this would all pass, especially if he didn't get on with a fire department in a year or two.

Nope. After the first two rejection letters, he just dyed his hair platinum-blond as a way of dealing with his disappointment.

As time went on, my heart began to really ache for him. I can still remember that sick feeling of watching my husband open a letter from the city, a letter that would determine our next steps as a family. Because he wanted this so badly, I couldn't help but have a change of heart about this whole thing. I started to really hope he'd get his dream job.

Ultimately, after staying the course all those years, Tom *finally* received a congratulations letter from the department he had been hoping for! I could not have been more proud.

Today, after being a once-reluctant fire wife, I'm happy to say that I am now an honored one, because not only do I share in my husband's life as a firefighter, I also have a rewarding life and purpose apart from his profession.

Looking back now at the challenges we faced, not to mention the fear and resentment I felt when he decided to become a firefighter, I'm now able to see that with an optimistic mindset, some flexibility, and trust, life *always* has a way of working itself out. As it turns out, though we did not follow the road in life I thought we would, the side-streets we experienced were better than I had imagined.

Introduction

If you have knowledge, let others light their candles in it.
MARGARET FULLER

Why I Wrote This Book

It took me nearly seven years to complete this book, but I was compelled to write it. And though it went through many rewrites as the years of experience and rough times changed us, I see now that when I started writing, I was too young and unseasoned as a fire wife to be of true encouragement to others.

When I began writing this book, my husband and I hadn't really been all that tested in our fire marriage yet. It wasn't until we entered our eighth year of my husband being a firefighter that we were slammed with some really heavy-duty challenges. These challenges changed not only how I felt about being a fire wife, but sometimes, in my darkest moments, made me honestly wonder whether we could continue as a fire couple.

When we faced our first real challenges as a fire couple, I couldn't find much in the way of support books to help us along. Toni Morrison, author and Nobel prize winner in literature, once said, "If there is a book you really want to read, but it hasn't been written yet, then you must write it." So, I did.

It has also been said that what you choose to teach is what you most need to learn, and let me tell you, I needed to learn a lot! Therefore, I did a great deal of research, plenty of reading, talked to a few successful fire couples, and then went about applying what I had learned to my own marriage to see if it worked—and guess what? It did. Most of what you read in this book is from my own personal experience as well as the experience of other fire couples. Do note that most names, where used, have been changed to respect the account-giver's privacy.

Today, after a whole lot of work and lots of rough patches, I can say that my firefighter and I are enjoying a great marriage. Though it is far from perfect, I am happy with where we are and proud of all we've come through.

I have also figured out that because fire couples don't have regular partnerships, we can't apply regular therapy. We need marriage counseling and information that is specific to what fire couples can expect to go through and what we can do to get back on track. I hope that you will find some of that in this book.

Finally, let me say that I wanted to write a book that was fire-wife focused. Though this book is primarily about building a solid partnership, the most important relationship you will ever have is the one that you have with yourself. Hence, it was really important to me that I write about all of it: your relationship, your life, and your dreams.

My Hope for You

It's my hope that this book will both reassure you and give you confidence, regardless of where you are in your fire-relationship and your life right now. Whether things are currently going well, or you're feeling discouraged and desperate, you *can* get through the tough stuff, achieve a happy union, and live a life that is equally satisfying to you both.

Of course, I can't forget that there's a whole other group of people inside our firefighter community: our female firefighters. They, too, face unique stresses in trying to balance their life with their relationships and career. While I wanted to write stories to benefit them as well, the truth is, I can only write and speak from my experiences. And because I literally do not know what it's like to walk in their shoes, it would have been extremely presumptuous of me to claim that my advice will pertain directly to them and their partners as well.

If, however, there is some insight to be gleaned or, better yet, it starts the conversation and inspires people to write about their own experiences, I would be overwhelmingly grateful—we all would be. The first-responder world needs more words of influence and insight from our women.

My Goal for This Book

What I want more than anything for fire couples reading my book is to truly appreciate what each person in a fire marriage goes through. I want fire wives to empathize with their partners and I want firefighters to empathize with their wives. It is only then that we can be there for each other. The reason why so many marriages end in divorce is because too many of them lack both an understanding and compassion for the other. Being self-absorbed in a relationship, especially in a fire one, is a recipe for disaster.

The other thing I want you to keep in mind is that although I'm writing about how to keep your fire partnership together, you will still have exclusive relationship issues all your own. In other words, every relationship has its own personality. Hopefully, however, in sharing my experience with you, this book will be a source of comfort, support, and optimism for you on your journey.

The core of this book is about getting to the *root* of what we need to make fire relationships succeed. I will speak often about our personal mindsets and attitudes. I will explore the common differences between men and women, the predictable rough patches you are guaranteed to go through, and provide some simple tools and suggestions to champion you over the hurdles.

Additionally, because long-term relationships force us to grow as individuals, I want to invite you to look deep within yourself: to heal any old patterns (mindsets, attitudes, personality traits, and any bottled-up stuff) that don't serve your self-esteem or life purpose.

If you don't know it yet, you'll soon come to realize that you are a truly powerful influence in your relationship. It's not always easy being with a firefighter, but once you reflect on the challenges and solutions, and understand that what you experience as a couple is normal, you will face trials with less fear and more of a "yes, we can!" attitude.

Our firefighters rely on us, their wives, so by you taking steps towards maintaining and having a great partnership, your spouse will be inclined to do the same.

I like what American author John Steinbeck says about understanding one another: "Knowing a man well never leads to hate and almost always leads to love."

The same goes for us as women. Let us build a bridge to understanding each other.

Table of Contents

Table of Contents

CHAPTER ONE

Firefighting
As Your Partner's Profession

*If there is any one secret of success, it lies in the ability to get
the other person's point of view and see things from that
person's angle as well as your own.*

HENRY FORD

How Knowing What They Do Will Benefit You Both

I got a phone call this morning from my husband, and I could barely understand a thing he said. He was exhausted, having just been up all night at a call. I'd been busy on this particular morning, doing what I do every morning: getting the kids off to school, making breakfast, tending to laundry, making lunch, and trying to find my workout gear for the gym.

"Speak up," I told him. "I can't hear you."

"We were at a big fire last night—have you watched the news?"

"No, but I'll turn it on."

My gut tightened when I saw the scene. Oh my God, this was why he hadn't called to say goodnight. It had been a burning apartment building, fully engulfed. The scene made my panic of a morning look like a Hawaiian day at the beach.

1

Just a few days earlier, these firefighters, our very good friends, were having a beer and a laugh while renovating our basement, and now this? On the news I could see their last names across their turnout gear as they saved people's lives. While I'd spent last night watching *The Bachelor*, my husband and his brothers were heading into this blazing apartment fire, wearing probably 50 pounds of equipment on their bodies, to bring people out to safety.

It was then I heard simultaneously from my husband and the reporter on television, "Seven-year-old boy." My heart sank. These are the worst kind of calls.

Our friend Doug brought the little boy out of the burning building. The television crews panned anguished faces. On the screen, I saw one of our friends working tirelessly over his little body. Writing this still brings tears to my eyes. Seventy percent of this young boy's body was burned; to tell you the truth, I can't remember if he succumbed to his injuries.

Our firefighters witness death often. Sometimes it's a medical call, other times a car accident, or, as in the above story, a fire and injuries.

Over a period of two weeks, I knew my husband had crawled through a window to help an isolated quadriplegic get up off the bathroom floor, assisted an elderly person in her filthy house because she could not get around on her own, and aided a frantic woman banging on the fire hall door who needed help because she'd been beaten by her boyfriend. Even when matters aren't life-and-death, our firefighters are involved when tensions are at their highest.

Wear and Tear and a Dream Come True

In his book, *Extreme Heat: A Firefighter's Life*, Canadian author and firefighter Jimmy Allen tells the reader in a forthright manner what it's like to be a firefighter. He describes in deep detail some of the harsher calls his crew went on. At times, I couldn't put his book down, and then there were other times when I had to. His blunt, no-nonsense style of writing and his tell-it-like-it-is personality really opened my eyes to the life of a firefighter. It made me want to be an even better support to my husband who, like many firefighters, rarely talks about everything he sees out there in the field.

Just think about what that does to a person; how it affects them when their psyche piles up with one gruesome, exhausting call after another. Now imagine being woken out of a dead sleep to ringing alarms several times a night to run out to those 911 calls? Personally, I would be a mess if I lived that life.

I asked my husband the other day if calls ever stay with him, and he told me that sometimes images come into his head out of the blue. Is it any wonder, then, why these guys have to joke around, play pranks, and otherwise use humor as a coping mechanism? I think if they are too sensitive about all that they see, they'll have a breakdown. Sadly, of course, some of them still do.

So then, why do they do it? With all that they know about what can happen to their mind, body, and spirit, why do they insist on running *into* a burning building when everyone else is running *out*?

The bottom line is that being a firefighter is a true life calling. Similar to those who are clergy, social advocates, doctors, and volunteers who travel to distant countries to tend to the sick and build houses for the poor, it's their passion. When a person becomes a firefighter, it's a privilege, an honor, and to many it's the best job in the world. So even with all the stress and challenges (health and otherwise), most firefighters will tell you that they love what they do.

It certainly takes a unique drive to become a firefighter; they're a special breed. My admiration for what they do is tremendous. They are an elite club of heroes. They were born to serve.

In the Beginning

Early in our marriage, I really lacked understanding for my husband's profession. Sometimes I'd even feel irritated when I'd see him napping yet again or acting cranky after a night shift. After all, I'd just spent the day looking after the kids, cleaning the house, and working part-time, and I really missed having a companion I could talk to at the end of the day.

But then something happened.

As I began to do research for this book, I realized I had been missing the critical knowledge of what it is that firefighters go through every day. I came to appreciate all that my husband and his coworkers do out there in the world. My sympathy grew when I realized not only how physically demanding his job is, but also how emotionally and mentally draining it is too.

Once I totally absorbed what he did while he was away from home, I was able to look at our relationship differently. It is my hope to provide you with some small part of that knowledge towards understanding your partner's career.

Some People Think Firefighting Is Cushy

Any fool can know. The point is to understand.
ALBERT EINSTEIN

Firefighters get teased a lot by those who aren't in the fire service, even from family and friends. Comments can range from "they're just lazy," to "they think they know everything," or even, "all they do is cook and eat." In fact, just this past summer, a relative of ours made a rather cruel comment behind my husband's back about his profession.

Though we as wives can get pretty annoyed by some of these more ignorant comments, our firefighters usually take it well, since they're used to getting teased ruthlessly by their brothers and sisters back at the hall.

The reality, however, is that firefighting is extremely hard work and it takes very smart men and women to do the job. After all, they have to be skilled in math, chemistry, and physics (with a college education to prove it!) to get on the job in the first place. Then they also need to remain calm in excruciatingly dangerous situations, communicate clearly to their team, and still be an excellent cook on top of all that!

My youngest son had the fortunate experience to spend the day at work with his father. Throughout the day, my husband kept sending me photos of our charming teen in his turnout gear, rappelling down a building and wielding the water hoses, all while smiling under the guidance of his very proud father. I loved getting those photos, and I also knew that my fourteen-year-old son was pretty excited when he saw what the guys were making them for lunch, too.

When my son Liam got home, he looked at me very seriously and said, "Mom, Dad has a really hard job ... I can't believe what he has to go through. He has to crawl on his hands and knees in a smoky building and look for someone when he can't even see. I feel sorry for him, Mom, because he never comes home and tells us what's going on."

Though my son is right, a firefighter can't exactly go to a cocktail party like people in other professions to regale the roomful of guests with stories of his profession. Oh, I can just see the sickened faces now.

Singer Ed Robinson, of the famous band Barenaked Ladies, once had a show on TV called *Ed's Up*, a series that had him try out different jobs for a day. When the time came to give him hands-on experience as a firefighter, Ed worked at Station 30 in Cleveland, Ohio. A night cam was focused on Ed as he was jarred out of a dead sleep time and time again, for both really big emergencies and some very little, annoying ones, too. In addition, he had to roll hose and keep the hall immaculate.

By the end of Ed's shift, he was not only hurting physically but he was indescribably exhausted. By the show's end, he couldn't say enough about what our firefighters do—and how they should get paid a whole lot more.

So, when you have friends who put their digs in about your firefighter, just remember this: in the big picture of life, it doesn't matter. What matters is your commitment to your relationship and, if you have any children, to your family. Instead of worrying about proving others wrong, focus on where your energy needs to be—such as with you, your partner, and maintaining a healthy relationship. And don't forget to laugh!

Now, that's not to say I don't occasionally throw in a trauma story or two to shut a few people up. The fact is, some people are just uninformed, and possibly even a little jealous. Not everyone has found their purpose in life, and they can get a little envious when they see someone else loving what they do. As my husband jokingly says when he gets teased, "Jealousy will get you nowhere."

But one thing I do know for certain is that all of those who choose to make light of what our men and women do for a living wouldn't last an hour with them on a call. Your partner wouldn't change their profession for the world, so stand grand and simply know that deep down it's all fun and games—until someone needs to call on your hero for help.

Firefighter Health

While our firefighters may love their job, the downside, of course, is that they are regularly exposed to a large number of toxic substances, horrific accidents, and sleep disturbances. As such, they are at risk for developing some devastating occupational illnesses like cancer, depression, post-traumatic stress disorder (PTSD), cardiovascular disease, noise-induced hearing loss, and pulmonary disease, just to name a few.

Here in our city, it is mandatory for our firefighters to get regular physicals and fitness tests. In places where it isn't, it is highly recommended, and I can't emphasize its importance enough.

Mental health is also a concern since our firefighters regularly witness trauma. When trauma is experienced every day and not dealt with, the mental distress can result in depression, PTSD or, worse, suicide. This is why we, as their partners, have to really encourage our firefighters to seek out time to de-stress, play sports, work out, have a spiritual life, and, if possible, schedule regular counseling sessions. This will support them in processing all the stuff that they see and experience.

When our firefighters process their experiences into a healthy mindset, they can learn to see themselves not just as responders to tragedy, but more affirmatively as protectors and rescuers to so many.

Shift Work: Hell on the Mind, Body, and Spirit

The only time I ever had to do shift work was when I had my two baby boys and got up in the middle of the night to feed them. Even with the fact that I had always been an energetic morning person, those nights, as so many new parents can attest to, are extremely grueling. Every day, I woke up sleep-deprived, fragile, and confused as to what day it was! I also had days when I felt scattered, forgetful, or blue.

"Of course you're blue," my friend said, "you've had no sleep!"

A lack of sleep from shift work, or from any work, impairs our cognitive function and yes, that can make us depressed.

Knowing that my symptoms were the result of little sleep, I knew that eventually my problems would dissipate when the boys finally slept through the night. However, "many shift workers find that they never fully adapt to their schedules and deal with disturbed sleep on an ongoing basis" (*Psychology Today* online magazine, written by John Klein, PhD, January 4, 2010, https://www.psychologytoday.com).

In her book, *The Sleep Revolution*, author, businesswoman, and co-founder of *The Huffington Post* Arianna Huffington brought the importance of sleep to the forefront. She describes how in 2007—because she was severely exhausted—she collapsed in her office, hit her head, broke her cheekbone, and lay in a pool of blood. Yes, a lack of sleep is very serious.

Sadly, when our firefighters run themselves ragged and don't make up for lost sleep at home, they can, like Arianna Huffington, get themselves into considerable trouble with the increased risk of accidents and poor job performance. Science has also proven that a chronic lack of sleep can negatively affect health. Heart attacks and diabetes are just a couple of serious health problems that can occur when a person never catches up on their sleep after working shifts.

Frequent Adrenaline Rushes and Their Horrible Side Effects

Have you ever felt frustrated with your partner because of their seeming lack of connection with you, their zombie-like behavior, or forgetfulness? Well, you should take the time to thank the real culprit—your partner's chronic adrenaline rushes, which strike every time those alarms ring for them to go on a call.

While adrenaline is exactly what jolts a firefighter up in the middle of the night to go out and save people, it is yet another source of unfortunate physical and mental side effects. Prolonged over a period of time, they not only cause our firefighters to crash and act like zombies, but frequent adrenaline rushes can also blow out their adrenal glands and cause memory loss.

So, what are our firefighters to do? And what are we as fire wives to do? The truth of the matter is, catching up on sleep is the most obvious cure. This is why, when my husband gets home, I urge him to hit the hay, knowing he'll be in a far better state of mind after a good snooze.

In addition to having a good sleep, your firefighter should have both their cortisol and testosterone levels tested, since they dip big time when they're under stress. When cortisol and testosterone levels are out of whack, a man (women too, by the way) will feel exhausted. To get a complete list of what should be checked, please consult with your doctor or naturopath.

Another great investment to facilitate wellness is to get inside an infrared sauna. Better yet, it's a great investment for fire halls around the country! Infrared saunas have been around for several years, and they are quite incredible.

After going to a fire, an infrared sauna is a great way for our firefighters to detox from all the smoke and chemicals they've absorbed through their skin. When my husband comes home to use ours after a fire, he wipes a layer of black soot off his body thanks to the sweating process.

Yoga is another great way to combat sleep deprivation: it clears the mind and relaxes the body, so our firefighters can fall asleep more easily. It's become super-popular with the firefighters at our department. The classes they go to all have funny names like "Yoga for Stiff Old Men!"

In the end, methods like massage, hydration, magnesium, and being in a cool, dark room are far healthier ways to fall asleep than prescribed sleeping pills, which can cause blackouts and are an absolute nightmare to get off of. If your firefighter (or you) needs a sleep aid for the short-term, try something natural from the health food store or some light, off-the-shelf medication from the drugstore.

Sleep deprivation is no laughing matter, so understanding that your spouse's shift work can really affect them is the key to understanding the need to come down, recover lost sleep, and maybe be on their own for a bit to "veg out."

Politics and Other Departmental Dramas

As much as you'll hear about how the majority of firefighters absolutely *love* their jobs, there is a very stressful side—apart from the 911 calls—that I'm sure you are pretty well aware of. I'm talking about politics and departmental drama.

Considerable turmoil can result from budget cuts, contract issues, or other problems with the city. And then there are situations like dealing with a substandard chief, observing malicious behaviors from those who play the system, or witnessing inconsistent policies that favour some people and reprimand others for image reasons.

These are not the only causes of insurmountable stress. All departments have witnessed tragedies when one of their brothers or sisters commits suicide, goes to rehab, or loses their job.

My husband had been on the job for several years when one of his best friends fell into alcohol and prescription medication abuse. Regrettably, his out-of-character behavior cost him his career and his house.

This ill-fated situation slammed like a tsunami into our home and others' because, for almost two years, my husband and his loyal firefighter friends had kept an eye on their fallen friend's mental health, taking him to appointments with counselors and lawyers. My husband completely missed two of our son Brayden's high school years while dealing with this situation. At the same time, my husband's mother passed away, so it was a very stressful and all-consuming time for us.

Eventually, however, we will all be touched by the unavoidable office politics and departmental dramas that come with your partner being on the job. Sometimes, these events are fairly inconsequential, and other times they are damn serious.

Fortunately, the links between mental health, the dangers of prescription drug overuse, and the horrific side effects of PTSD are finally getting some much-needed attention.

Once again, early intervention is key to prevent your partner from going down any of these dark roads. To this day, the wife of our fallen friend beats herself up for not preventing her husband from going to work on a night when she knew something was wrong.

If you notice a potential situation that could threaten your firefighter or their job—if your spouse is acting strangely, or if their behavior has changed—then you have to trust your instincts. Put your foot down, talk to them, and get assistance from your fire friends and family. You don't want an intervention of any kind to be a matter of hindsight.

Signs of Trauma, Critical Stress, and PTSD

PTSD was first diagnosed during World War I in soldiers suffering the aftereffects of war. It was originally called "shell shock." If you watch some of the old films that they took of soldiers suffering from shell shock, it would give you chills. When people have PTSD, they are stuck emotionally from trauma, and can't seem to get out of the mental turmoil that has built up from having experienced it.

Because I am neither a health care professional nor a certified therapist who deals with PTSD, I won't be covering this disorder in great detail. It's such a complex area of mental health, and the reality is that there are so many professional debates surrounding PTSD and how to heal it. There are, however, some online websites that I think are useful for PTSD; these can be found in the Appendix of this book. Furthermore, there are opportunities for first responders themselves to take courses that support and counsel their brothers and sisters who are indeed suffering from this debilitating disorder.

Recently I read a study in *Science Today* that nine out of ten firefighters suffer from some form of Post-Traumatic Stress Syndrome, despite it being greatly underreported. The lack of reporting and general information available about just how many of our firefighters suffer from PTSD tells me that the study hasn't always been a top priority. Fortunately, things are changing. Taking the stigma out of seeking relief should be our top priority.

I personally cannot imagine dealing with trauma day in and day out. Twice in my life I have witnessed horrible accidents. One was of a man who'd been thrown from a car; I'll never forget the sight of his head impaled in a telephone pole, his feet and legs all twisted. Another time I was asked to assist with cardiopulmonary resuscitation (CPR) on a construction worker at my office building; he died later on.

In both cases, after witnessing the accident, I slipped into a deep sadness that I couldn't shake for days. I still get overwhelmingly affected whenever I hear of a tragedy or see an accident. However, my spouse and yours witness this sort of devastation routinely, so it's bound to take its toll.

While some firefighters are pretty adept at alleviating their suffering bonding with friends over a firehouse meal, pulling pranks on each other, or talking things over with their partners, not all of them are able to process their trauma.

When your firefighter is affected by trauma—and really, it's only a matter of time before they are to some extent—it's imperative that you as their partner see their change in behavior as a cry for help rather than as a personal attack on you. If stress or PTSD are left unchecked, your relationship will definitely suffer for it.

Here are just a few of the warning symptoms to look out for: insomnia, reliving a tragic event, depression, outbursts of anger, excessive drug or alcohol use, feelings of extreme guilt, withdrawing from friends and activities they used to enjoy, emotional detachment, paranoia, and recklessness. Getting outside treatment for your partner when they may be experiencing some of the above issues will help them to work through what they are suffering.

Counseling is something I believe we all ought to utilize from time to time anyhow, not just when we get mentally or emotionally out of control. Keeping up with a counselor, a life coach, or a spiritual advisor such as a pastor can give us the tools to use during emotional times, such as when we have big life decisions to make.

In getting people to talk about themselves, a professional can facilitate them through life's upsets with clarity and compassion. More importantly, they facilitate people in a way that helps them to garner their own inner wisdom and solutions.

Telephone or Tell a Firefighter

If you haven't figured it out already, you soon will: firefighters are a gossipy bunch. Though I'm sure not everyone is a story-spreader, I cannot for the life of me figure out why this is so prevalent in departments.

For the most part when I was growing up, the boys around me did not talk about other people; it was just not something guys were known to do. Imagine my surprise when I became aware of this fire hall habit!

Here is my advice to you: if you do not want to have the entire department weigh in on your relationship issues, then you really need to watch who you talk to and ask your partner to zip their lips. I went absolutely mad when I found out my husband had spoken about our marital issues around the lunch table at the hall with the goal of supporting another firefighter.

The problem is that what is said at the hall doesn't stay in the hall. And what may have been some well-meaning advice to one of his brothers was turned into fodder for some of the guys to tell their wives, and then the wives to tell their friends ... and so on.

Talk to your partner, as I had to, about keeping mum when it comes to some more personal challenges in your relationship. Otherwise, although they may just be seeking out or giving advice, this tidbit can be used by some of the recipients for juicy gossip. It's hard enough going through rough patches with a firefighter without having a whole bunch of people weigh in on—or make light of—what you're going through.

On the bright side, it seems gossip is now being addressed in some fire departments through sensitivity training. One motto that really stood out to my husband was "The standard you walk past is the standard you accept."

Until the culture changes, it's best to remember that if you don't want anything to get out, don't say anything. A culture of gossip is damaging, no matter how you dress it up or try to make it look acceptable. As they say in politics, it's just lipstick on a pig.

The Need for Control and Order

While not all firefighters are tidy, they certainly all have their areas where they need a sense of order. Otherwise, they'll turn into the supervisor from hell and demand that "this get organized right away." It could be their man-cave, the workout room, or even the utensil drawer.

I will admit to feeling a little insecure about this, because the fire hall trumps me in the organizational department hands-down. Transitioning from the clean-and-orderly hall to the home, where real life happens, can be an adjustment.

So, what do I do personally?

Well, it took me some time to figure it out, but after my husband's night shifts, for my own sanity I started keeping "his areas" and "his walkway" tidy. That way when he arrives home, he walks right through his uncluttered little route and goes straight up to bed. Hey, a peace-lover has to do what a peace-lover has to do.

My sister Keeli had a really good point about this control issue, and not in a bad way. The reason why your firefighter needs a sense of order might be because firefighters never know what to expect when they go to work. They don't know what time the calls will come in, how many times they'll be woken up in the night or called out during the day. They don't know what they'll see or what tragedies they will be faced with.

When our partners don't have a sense of what chaos they can expect to be up against, needing to control some aspects of their lives becomes one way of managing things. It makes sense to me. Once we understand this "need," we can help our partners make the transition from hall to home a little easier for them and, of course, for the rest of us.

The Brotherhood Bond and Why It's Necessary

Brotherhood is the very price and condition of man's survival.
CARLOS P. ROMULO

One of the things I admire the most about our firefighters is the bond that they have with each other. Whenever I hear my husband talking on the phone to another firefighter, I always hear him end the conversation with "Hey, thank you, brother ... you got it, brother ... talk later, brother."

I completely appreciate, particularly if you are new to the firefighter life culture, that wrapping your head around this "brotherly bond" can be trying. This can be especially difficult when it seems as though they put their brothers and sisters at the hall before everything else. While it was hard for me in the beginning, what I have come to realize is that it isn't that my husband puts his brothers first—it's just that there is an immense loyalty between them.

When my husband was sick, our firefighter family's loyalty surpassed even our blood relatives. They showed up to fix our pool, they sat with my hubby in the hospital, and they did whatever else was needed during that time. I will never forget how much their reliability, kindness, and compassion meant to us. All it takes is a group text, and these guys show up. They are used to responding to emergencies—it's who they are.

Those days were very defining for me, particularly as a fire wife. They say that during times of hardship, you find out who your true family and friends are; and they are all of it.

The brotherhood bond is based on the values our firefighters share: honor, loyalty, service, trust, and teamwork. Combine that with the fact that they live, eat, and sleep under the same roof part-time, respond to serious emergencies together, and then deal with the after effects of those tragedies, it's only natural that a unique bond forms. And it's a powerful one: their lives literally depend on being able to trust each other in dangerous situations.

While I am my husband's wife and his support, I cannot even begin to fathom what they witness together when they head out to car accidents, suicides, and medical emergencies. These events are life-changing. The brotherhood bond is unbreakable, and they will always have each other's backs. We should all be so lucky.

When Your Lover's the Rookie and Why They Need to Be

When my husband finally got onto the fire department, we were elated. But being the rookie at the fire hall is a very stressful state. As the one at the very bottom of the fire pole, you not only have to be on your toes for alarms like everyone else, but also be the first one jumping up to answer the phone, clean toilets, do dishes, and, of course, be the receiver of some over-the-top pranks. Enduring a whole year of being a rookie meant that my husband was exhausted at the end of his shifts more often than not.

Being the rookie meant that there were also a lot of adjustments in our home. My husband took a pay cut (compared with his previous job) when he got hired as a firefighter with the city, and he wasn't allowed to work another job during that first year. As such, I worried about the lack of money coming in to support our young family.

Though it was a very demanding and financially tight time for us, I'd honestly never seen my husband so happy. The challenges of this one-year probation period were nothing compared to the five years of disappointment he experienced while trying to get on with the department of his dreams.

As time goes on and your partner gains some seniority, the pay checks will get fatter. And of course, there will always be other rookies to take their place! So, although this whole rookie thing was super disheartening for me as a rookie's wife, I came to realize that this probation period is a very important part of the process.

Being a firefighter is not an easy job, so "jumping up to answer the phone" is practice for what is to come (having to jump out of bed in the middle of the night or up from the table when dinner has just been served to go to an emergency); firefighters need to be quick on their toes.

It's also essential that any rookie on the job knows their place in the line of command, because listening to their superiors is imperative. Without being able to follow orders, a firefighter will not last. This boot camp initiation is what builds a firefighter's grit and keeps them humble.

Respect is a huge factor in the fire department, so a rookie needs to know the rules of the fire hall even before they get there. Eventually your firefighter will get the hang of how things are run and will benefit from it in the long term.

There is no room for cockiness in the fire department, especially from the new recruit. A firefighter builds their reputation with others from the get-go, and a good one is worth its weight in gold. Besides, the more people who respect them in the department, the more support they'll get from brothers and sisters in the years to come. Firefighters do not suffer fools.

A Special Kind of Family

Having observed my husband's and Uncle Ron's relationships with their "brothers," I've concluded that dysfunctional families

19

could take a page or two from how these firefighters interact with each other on a day-to-day basis.

That's not to say there isn't still a whole lot of brotherly and sisterly dysfunction at the hall, but from what I've experienced over the years, these firefighters know how to connect and have fun when they get together.

Here's what I learned about family from our firefighters:

They Spend Fun Time Together: These guys are active and like to have fun. So next time you have a family gathering, instead of just sitting around a table waiting for one dysfunctional relative to say something rude to another dysfunctional relative, think of something fun to do. Play cards or a trivia game, go fishing, bowling, play soccer, or get a game of road hockey going. When people are actively interacting, there is less time to focus on the negative traits of others.

They Have a Cause: Firefighters are renowned for their charity work, so why not find something purposeful for your family to dedicate themselves to? Maybe get together once a year to make soup as a Soup Sister or Broth Brother (www.soupsisters.org), collect clothes for the homeless, have a book drive, or go on a run to raise money for an important cause. Families thrive when they have a common goal they can share.

They Cook and Eat Together: Everyone knows that firefighters are famous for their superb meals. Cooking together is a great way to teach others how to cook, but also to spend time together and talk. When we prepare a meal with our family, it's a great time to bond and relax ... chopping is very therapeutic!

When I used to bake with my children or my young niece and nephew, it was, unbeknownst to them, a math lesson in fractions—as well as a great time to teach them how to set the table and wash up. Why not take turns choosing something new to make, then all sit down to enjoy the fruits of your labor?

They Value Tradition: Firefighters are all about traditions. For me, tradition is what makes life meaningful and sacred. From ice skating parties to Christmas tree burnings to family BBQs complete with bouncy castles and horseback rides, when you are part of a fire department family, you can look forward to lots of annual fun.

One year, my husband and his crew were working on Father's Day, so the Captain thought it would be nice to make breakfast for the crews' families. They put up a dunk tank at the hall, made a spectacular brunch, and the kids got to climb the fire trunk and do a ton of other fun things. Traditions and rituals create fond memories.

They Work as a Team: The way these guys work together fascinates me: they have such a well-organized system down. My mom and her siblings were the same when it came to getting their house prepared for company. Everyone just pitched in until the work was done.

When people learn to work together as a team, we learn about being flexible, helping one another, and seeing what gifts other people bring to the table. And, of course, many hands make lighter work, right?

They Know How to Lighten Up and Have Fun: People who don't have enough to do in their life worry about unimportant things. As I mentioned, knowing what these guys regularly experience has put life in general for me into proper perspective. Sometimes, families can get too serious by judging each other or bitching about little issues. I love that our firefighters treat most problems with a large dose of humor and then get on with it.

My husband used to love working with his now-retired friend Captain Mark Togno. Mark made life at the hall super fun and taught the guys all about the balance of work and play during a shift. They had the important work and training time, but he also knew how essential it was to refresh the mind, body, and spirit with some fun. He would often get a game of ball going out in the courtyard.

My husband would come home in such a good mood after being under the direction of this captain. Lightening up and having fun is the perfect balance to the more harrowing things people go through in life.

They Take Sensitivity Training: When a person takes sensitivity training, they are learning to be aware of how their words and actions can negatively impact another person. Imagine how many more families would get along if they were thoughtful in how they treated their siblings, children, and parents?

Sensitivity training is equivalent to self-reflection and considering the Golden Rule: Treat others as you would like to be treated.

They Forgive and Forget: Most of the time when there's an issue between firefighters the end game is to clear the air and then move on to the business of saving lives. Being unified to work together efficiently as a team is the cornerstone of the fire service.

Forgiving is, essentially, letting it go. You don't have to like someone personally; you just stop spending your time resenting them and move on. If more families learned to forgive and forget, there'd be less division and more unity.

CHAPTER TWO

Marriage and Divorce

You think being a firefighter is tough?
Try being married to one.

ANONYMOUS

Why Do Fire Marriages Fall Apart?

I love this quote. And yes, while I love my firefighter and for the most part life is sweet, let's be honest here: regular life and regular marriages have their challenges; being married to a firefighter is a challenge all its own.

Just in this past year alone, both my husband and I have counted at least five fire marriages that have broken down and ended in either separation or divorce. So then, here's the million-dollar question: why is it that some fire marriages fall apart?

Well, as in most divorces, there are a myriad of reasons why couples break up: irreconcilable differences, adultery, addiction, and, of course, some people just grow apart. But in the fire department, as in most "military" lines of work, the sacrifices expected from the spouse of those in uniform can become unbearable.

When firefighters get home, they are so zapped mentally, emotionally, and physically from a day of emergencies that there isn't always much left to give their spouse. If that spouse takes this personally, they may start to feel neglected in their marriage.

Additionally, firefighters sleep a lot—and who could blame them? Trauma, shift work, and broken sleep will catch up with you. This, however, can begin to wear on a partner who's been busy sticking to the schedule, holding down the fort at home—possibly while working full-time—and being the only one available to drive junior to lacrosse practice, the dentist, or the emergency room.

Other contributing factors in fire divorces are that our heroes spend an awful lot of time away from home. Often they're working at the hall, going to their second job, or filling in a shift for a co-worker who wants to go to their kid's soccer game or ballet recital. They also shake a boot in front of a liquor store to raise money for muscular dystrophy, the burn fund, or some other worthy cause; then they go and play hockey, fish, or otherwise relax with their fire siblings to blow off steam and try to erase the images of last night's fatal car accident.

Sometimes, infidelity may rear its ugly head (from either the firefighter or their partner). Of course, like marriages all over the world, this is not isolated to just firefighters. But while I do believe that infidelity is a character issue, let's be honest: everyone loves a firefighter. All you have to see is how some women behave when they're near any of the guys in the firefighter calendar. You might just have to pick your chin up off the floor. It's startling.

In the case of one firefighter's divorce, it was his addiction to drugs and alcohol that put an end to his marriage and, temporarily, the career he loved. Drugs and alcohol can ruin lives, but some feel it is the quickest way to deal with the disturbing things they see on the job. Of course, many addictive behaviors are simply a Band-Aid for a much bigger issue.

Divorce and a Look into Its Future

First of all, let me be clear about one thing. I do not believe that anyone should stay in a relationship if there's violence, abuse in the home, or if the children are being affected negatively without a resolution. Nor do I believe anyone should stay in a marriage where there is an addiction wreaking havoc on the family and not being treated.

I do feel though, apart from these things, that divorce has become an easy way out for too many people. In fact, while studies vary, one survey that was reported by the Daily Mail in August of 2014, "asked 2,000 UK men and women who got divorced if they'd regretted their decision and a whopping 50% of these divorcees said they had regrets."

One of the gravest mistakes people make when they entertain the idea of divorce is thinking that the grass will be greener on the other side of the fence. Well, I've got news for you. My friends who have been divorced will tell you that it's not. In fact, any problems that you have with your current partner, you can plan to have with your next one, too. Once the honeymoon stage wears off, and trust me it will, you will revisit the same old set of problems you had with spouse number one, only this time with a brand-new person.

As well, just imagine and consider the financial issues you can expect. Oh, sure, your spouse will pay support to you—or you to them—but maybe now they're involved in a new relationship, have a couple more kids with this new partner, and feel strapped trying to support not just their old family, but the new one, too.

In addition to the financial issues, there will be emotional ones. A couple good friends who are in blended family situations have shared with me some of the difficulties they face. For instance, if your children have to share you or your ex (who barely has that much time as it is), there will be jealousy and hurt feelings. This happens especially around birthdays and holidays, since now there's a whole other group of people: new step-parents, their new step-siblings, the new partner's ex-partner, and so on.

Of course, you will still have to consider your ex's busy schedule and shift work. If you thought it was tough before, just take a moment to picture what it would be like with two separate homes and two separate families.

How Divorce Affects Firefighters and the Department

The problem is, unless a wife verbally tells her firefighter she's unhappy in their marriage and offers up a step-by-step plan, many times, because of their crazy schedule and sleep deprivation, firefighters won't tune in. This isn't to cut them down in any way, because I think they're amazing. It's just that the realities of their job—high stress, emotionally draining, sleep depriving, and long hours away from the home—can cause their normal intuition on more intimate issues to become dampened.

Therefore, when a fire wife leaves her partner, even after years of being unhappy, more often than not they are floored, to say the least. She may have nagged or bitched and thrown in a few silent treatments over the years, but if the issues weren't spelled out clearly for both partners, a firefighter may feel blind-sided.

Men, in particular, don't often do divorce well. Emotionally, women tend to move on a little easier, perhaps because they generally have the support of family and friends who get them through. However, you certainly don't have to go far to see what divorce does to a firefighter.

To firefighters, their wives are everything. They may have a bunch of coworkers they are tight with, and they might get off track now and then by spending too much time away from home, but for your own firefighter you are their lover, their routine, and their soft place to fall. You are their best friend.

When anyone divorces or otherwise loses a long-term partner, they can be emotionally devastated. Here are just some of the effects divorce has on emotional, mental, and physical health:

- angry, resentful
- isolation
- poor eating habits
- increased drug or alcohol use
- poor work performance
- cognitive decline
- stress and heart disease
- depression, anxiety
- increased suicide rates

Now, considering all those side effects, remember that a firefighter has to now get out there and save someone's life. The profession of firefighting requires that anyone on the job be sober, clear-thinking, and a mentally- and emotionally-healthy person who can stay alert in order to save other people's lives in risky situations.

The irony, of course, is that although our firefighters are trained for high-pressured emergencies of every sort, most wouldn't have a 911 answer on how to save their own marriages.

Firefighters train innumerable hours in rope rescue and hazmat, giving their lives over to perfect strangers every day, but they devote not a single minute to the stresses they and their spouses will feel once they surrender their lives to the fire department.

If our firefighters had relationship training on the job, it might save the fire department a fortune in stress leave, rehabilitation, and costly, dangerous accidents.

Supporting this point, a Canadian survey from a research piece (The Risks and Rewards of Marriage for Firefighters: A Literature Review With Implications for EAP, August 2016) said that the 50% of firefighters found "maintaining a relationship with one's romantic partner" a highly stressful part of the job. The good news, however, is that this old-boy battalion has slowly recognized the need for counselling and mental health care in recent years and because of that, divorce amongst male firefighters appears to have decreased: firedeptfamily.com/firefighter-divorce-rates. Hopefully implementing relationship instruction into their training will be next.

You Married a Firefighter or Are Planning to Marry One

One of my good friends, who is at this moment a single, male firefighter, told me once, "Whenever I meet a woman, I never tell her I'm a firefighter right away. Instead, I'll let her think my side job is all I do." In his case, that's his job as a construction worker.

"Why is that?" I asked him.

He told me that firefighters often attract "groupie" types who pursue firefighters without seriously considering the reality of being in a firefighter relationship or whether their personality is suited to being a fire spouse.

And the truth is, those who blindly get into a relationship with a firefighter without taking an honest, hard look at the stresses they'll have to face are in for a rude awakening. Too many people, as it turns out, can become enamored by the hero fantasy and the uniform. They never stop to consider the challenges of being married to someone in this profession.

In addition to a partner going blindly into a fire marriage, a firefighter may find themselves equally flattered by the attention they get from such a groupie type, not taking into consideration if they've even got the character to be their spouse. It goes both ways.

Through his discernment and wisdom, my friend will probably have a very successful marriage one day. By not telling women upfront that he is a firefighter, he is able to weed out the "groupies" from the women who are much better suited to go the distance with him. I think if more firefighters did this, there would probably be fewer firefighter divorces.

Anyone who is going to marry a firefighter (or who may be already married to one) must strengthen certain innate qualities if they are going to stay that way. A fire wife must be independent and compassionate, flexible to a constantly-changing schedule, strong enough to stand her ground, and above all have a sense of humor.

Top Ten Truths About My Fire Marriage

These ten core truths about my marriage to my firefighter are kind of like my very own serenity prayer: it reminds me to put my distinctive marriage into perspective and to also think big picture. If you'd like, try making a list of your own to glance at from time to time when you need to re-center yourself.

Truth Number 1: You have to understand, first and foremost, that firefighter families are not like other families: you are a unique couple, and you have to treat your relationship as such. Therefore, you cannot compare your relationship to, say, your sister's or your friend's.

Firefighters, as we know, have had an exorbitantly high divorce rate compared with other marriages, because their careers are highly stressful. And while other military-like families may understand what you go through, most others will not. Therefore, you must treat a fire relationship with a different pair of gloves.

Truth Number 2: Service and sacrifice will be at the heart of your relationship. Firefighters volunteer in the community, and most fire wives find themselves doing the same, either because they were people of service to begin with or they find themselves inspired to join their partner in serving the community.

Interestingly enough, when we focus on serving others, we can also find our own life's purpose. Sacrifice, in a balanced way, keeps us from becoming self-absorbed; being of service brings meaning to our lives.

Truth Number 3: You'll be self-reliant. All the things I used to leave up to my hubby before he became a firefighter, I've now taken into my own hands. Because of his shift work and recuperating time, if I want something done, I have to do it myself.

It's certainly given me a lot of confidence. After watching many YouTube tutorials, I've learned how to paint, spackle, and look after my car. Now if I could only learn to drywall ...

Truth Number 4: You're marrying into a really big family, and that can be annoying at times. I mean, they don't call each other "brother" and "sister" for no reason. Because of this big family atmosphere, it can sometimes feel overwhelming; someone is always competing for your partner's time, whether they need help with a project or they are going through a crisis or are asking to change shifts.

Having a big family, however, does have its advantages. Your day will come when you'll be super thankful, particularly if your partner needs help with a project or goes through a crisis. Even the kids benefit: mine have great memories of all of us camping together and going to all the big, fun, firefighter family events.

Truth Number 5: You'll need courageous levels of commitment. Maya Angelou once said that "courage is the most important of all virtues, because without courage you can't practice any other virtues consistently."

This powerful phrase will empower you, particularly when you are going through a rough patch. I've practiced courageous commitment many times with my husband, particularly when I felt like I couldn't go on with our marriage. Miraculously, it all worked out for the better!

Let courageous commitment be your mantra when you're fighting for the future you've worked so hard for already. Face relationship and life challenges with truth. Then, with courageous commitment, warrior your way through.

Truth Number 6: Whatever you focus on in your fire relationship will grow. This life law is a really important one to remember, particularly in a firefighter union where the demands can really stretch you. Deal with issues expeditiously so that you don't harbor any negativity or resentment.

Feed your relationship lots of good energy. Focus on what you love about your relationship and your life. Gratitude is key; count your blessings.

Truth Number 7: You will need humor. Nothing beats a good laugh when the going gets tough. And while humor is clearly not appropriate in every situation, it does lighten a heavy heart when you go through those rough patches in life. Our firefighters are masters of humor—they have to be with all the stuff they see.

Truth Number 8: You absolutely have to prioritize your relationship. Because you can both be pressed for time, it's easy to drift apart. There will always be events and invitations to pull you in a variety of directions; however, prioritizing time with your firefighter is time well-spent. Trust me, it's easier to maintain your relationship with quality time than it is to fix and repair it.

Truth Number 9: In addition to making your relationship a priority, you also have to make yourself a priority. When you are happy and fulfilled, your relationship will be, too.

Standing strong in your relationship, but also in your life and dreams, is necessary for personal happiness and inner peace. We all need purpose, and we all have a calling to complete. Making your relationship a priority is vital. However, making sure you fill your own heart and soul is more so.

Truth Number 10: Your fire relationship is not a romance novel. Rather, consider it a really great epic. When I was young, miniseries were really popular: *Roots, North and South, The Winds of War, The Thorn Birds.* Epics aren't sweet, lightweight stories; they are life-changing, powerful ones. They cover every life experience we, as human beings, can all relate to: from heartbreak and conflict to joy and intimacy.

We put undue pressure on our relationships when we treat them like a one-dimensional romance novel. I am here to joyfully report that no healthy partnership is wonderful all the time. There are life challenges and daily stresses you'll go through, so it's important that you don't compare yourself to some preconceived, made-up idea of how perfect your relationship should be. Think of your fire relationship as a story woven into a tapestry rich in experience, deepening love, and all that is real and true about life. What could be better than that?

CHAPTER THREE

Moving from Rough Water to Smooth Sailing

*When you get into a tight place and everything goes
against you, till it seems as though you could not hang
on a minute longer, never give up then, for that is just
the place and time that the tide will turn.*

HARRIET BEECHER STOWE

Pivotal Tools for Your Journey with Your Firefighter

One night my husband said, "Guess what ... I've been thirteen years on the job today!"

"Holy," I replied. "You mean I've survived being married to a firefighter for thirteen years?"

Of course, we had a laugh about that, since it wasn't the first reaction either one of us expected from me—it was, however, the first thought that came to mind. Though he'd been on the job for a magical thirteen, the two of us were going into our twenty-first year of marriage.

I've always said that my husband and I have had two marriages: one before firefighting, and one after it. "Oh my God," I said, "we used to be a nice, normal couple."

And yet, as my husband and I proceed through our marriage, I am thankful the two of us put the work in because, not unlike you, there have been periods when we each felt disillusioned and disappointed. Honestly, there were times I didn't know how we could be happy with each other again.

The most empowering thing about going through those marital rough patches is that the tools you uncover to use in your fire relationship during those times will not only give you assurance, but make you and your partner stronger and wiser.

The Art of Partnership

"You need to make a list," I said to my husband, "of everything that you need from me to make this marriage better. I'll make one too, so we can each see what we need."

"Why do we need lists?" he asked. I know he meant it as a question, but I heard it as an argument.

"Oh, here we go." I felt my stomach churn. "I can't just do this on my own," I pleaded. "You need to help here; we need to improve our marriage in so many areas."

But as he argued with me about putting "a lousy list" together, I just happened to notice that behind my hubby's argument was what looked like a seriously terrified man! A man who would probably rather lose a limb, or have the house's roof spontaneously cave in, than take an inventory of his feelings.

For some people, having a "talk about things" is comparable to how I would feel about being asked to step on a scale with a full audience in tow: sheer panic. If this is your partner, it doesn't mean they don't want things to get better. And if it's you, it's okay to be terrified. Just know that a serious relationship is going to require you to face those fears from time to time.

And keep this in mind: while you may feel vulnerable talking about how you feel or discussing more intimate issues with your partner, the more you practice it and make it a priority, the better you will get at it and the better you will feel. Be patient with yourself and with your partner.

More than anything, our partners want us to be happy in our relationships—and vice-versa. Therefore, when my hubby told me to "just give me a list of things you want me to change," he was serious. With his work, he doesn't have much emotional energy leftover for examining our relationship, and for the most part he's fine with the way things are ... of course, if he were to write his list it would probably include, "more sex, sex, and well, more sex."

Now, I don't want to downplay the importance of our firefighters' feelings and needs. It's just that they don't like the way we can sometimes complicate a relationship when their work life is already so complicated. And they are, for the most part, refreshingly uncomplicated. Just give them a plan and they'll naturally go about fixing it. Because that's what firefighters do: they fix things.

I remember the "needs requests" I'd given my husband in the past. When I told him once I wanted flowers more often, he ordered them in advance for the whole year so they'd come automatically and he wouldn't get in trouble for forgetting. When I told him he needed to be the homework sergeant with our teenage son at home, he stepped up to the plate.

Alas, my husband was more than willing to make our marriage better; he just needed me to provide him with a very detailed, comprehensive road map with plenty of directional signs to show him the way.

You, my dear fire wife, are in a better position to know what your marriage needs, so listen to your instincts, and then lead the way. Might this be exhausting? Yes. Is it fair? Not really, but nor can you expect your emotionally-drained firefighter to take on all of the relationship responsibility either. It's one of the unique challenges of a fire-relationship, and my reason for writing a book for us fire wives and not our firefighting partners. And so, in this chapter I have provided some practical suggestions for approaching your firefighter to solve conflicts and how to communicate your feelings to them for a win-win for both partners.

Make a Plan for Smoother Sailing

Here is a life law that you cannot change, no matter how much you may want to: "You will always harvest what *you* plant." If you want different life results, you've got to make different life choices. If you want to live higher, you've got to raise the bar. Here are things to think about before you make a plan for smoother sailing.

You Have to Choose: It all begins with a choice, right? If you want a happy relationship, then you've got to make that choice and be intentional with what you want.

You Have to Commit: We stand at the altar when we get married for a reason. We make a pledge before our family, friends, or an Elvis impersonator to love, honor, cherish, and commit. Whether you're still making your way to that altar or have already made your vows, once you make the choice to improve your relationship you've got to commit to it.

You Have to Communicate: It all begins with expressing to one another what it is you want and need. Silence will not reconcile.

Good, healthy communication also includes good listening. If we don't listen, we're not going to know what's going on in our partner's head.

You Have to Care: When we are going through a rough patch, it's very easy to objectify our spouse, and sometimes, not even see them as a human being. It's really important that we return to love with our spouse, and that means remembering that they hurt, too.

You Have to Connect: The goal in every partnership is to keep a connection between spouses. If, during a difficult time, we fail to reach that goal, reconnection is the key to recovery. That connection is our North Star, allowing us to navigate from rough seas to smooth sailing. When we feel connected to our spouse, we feel that all is well with the world.

Keep it Simple: As I already mentioned, while I do believe fire wives have tremendous influence in their relationship, I do think we have a tendency to over-complicate things when it comes to our firefighters. Understanding our differences is a necessary component on the path to marital success.

My Personal Tools for Smooth Sailing

When firefighters take courses to improve their skills on the job, they often use the toolbox analogy. That way, when a firefighter is in any emergency situation, they are prepared in advance. An instructor will ask, "What do you need in your toolbox for this scenario?"

The same toolbox analogy can be applied to your relationship. As a couple, specifically as a couple whose challenges are quite unique, knowing what's in your toolbox is a very wise thing indeed. That way, you know what you can use to navigate back to smooth sailing when your relationship encounters rough waters.

When I broke down all the steps my husband and I exercised on the road to reconciliation, I came up with the following tools:

1.   External Tools
2.   Connection Tools
3.   Internal Tools

External Tools

Words Have Power

Words are P-O-W-E-R F-I-L-L-E-D. You can use your words to build a person up and liberate them, or tear them down and ruin their self-esteem in one fell swoop. You can use them to push people away or bring them closer to you. There is nothing better than being around a person who is conscious of the words they speak.

Like you, I've been around people whose constant negativity, judgment, and criticism not only bring me down but wear me out. I feel weary after spending time with them. You spend a lot of time with your partner, hopefully for many years to come, so your relationship with them will flourish if you are mindful of your language.

The great thing about words is that they have the power to change lives. They can inspire people to improve; that is how powerful words are.

People who were brought up in negative homes might mistakenly believe that their chronic criticizing is just their way of being helpful. Well, it's not.

When my kids were growing up, I used strategies recommended by the Virtues Project (www.virtuesproject.com) to implement character building words—which they called 'virtues'—to acknowledge, thank, and correct them.

39

The Virtues Project is a global, grassroots initiative designed to inspire the practice of virtues. Their goal is to empower individuals to live more authentic, meaningful lives. If you need a list of virtues to start implementing in your own vocabulary to build people up positively and to recognize their gifts within, I highly recommend the Virtues Project.

Communication 101—What Works and What Doesn't

The definition of "communication" is the exchanging of information or news and the successful sharing of ideas and feelings in a dialogue or other connection. Effective communication does not include talking *at* people, dictating, yelling, or being demanding of them. Communicating well is an art form, and it takes work.

The irony is that while I may be a public speaker for a living, and can articulate myself clearly through written articles, I always need to work on my communication skills with my husband. Intimate relationships bring out a lot of raw emotions that we don't tend to encounter in other aspects of our lives.

Here are just some of the really bad communication styles that I've found, through personal experience, to not be beneficial:

Nagging: This is when a person continually complains or highlights faults without a solution in sight. When people nag, nobody listens.

Giving the Silent Treatment: Unless your partner is psychic, not speaking up won't get you anywhere—the same problems will just come up again and again.

Passive Aggressiveness: This is when you consistently avoid direct confrontation, either by communicating in an indirect manner or presenting indirect resistance when something's upsetting you. Resentment builds, then you explode!

Aggressiveness: This angry, in-your-face form of non-communication is quite off-putting. Many people feel unsafe when faced with aggressiveness. Being assertive by saying what you mean (and meaning what you say) is not the same as aggression: aggressiveness is being hostile, particularly with the intent to dominate.

On the other hand, when a person is assertive, they are composed and constructive when communicating their truth, whether standing up for others or standing up for themselves. We'll discuss more on how to communicate assertively in this chapter.

Talking to Everyone but Your Partner: This is also known as "triangulation." When you talk about your partner to everyone but them, they unknowingly get disrespected behind their back. More importantly, because they don't know what's going on, things can't change.

Rude Body Language and Tone: Rolling eyes, walking away when someone is speaking (body language), or being sarcastic, condescending, or rude (tone) are defensive tactics. They are ineffective as a form of communication because they fuel your partner's anger and only build walls between you.

Conflict Resolution

It's taken me a long time to become self-disciplined enough to know what works and what doesn't after my husband and I have had a disagreement. Now, whenever I need to talk to my man about something, I practice the following first:

41

Pick a Good Time: They say that timing is everything, and it is. I know that after a rough night at work is not a good time to talk to my hubby about anything. When he tries to talk about finances just as we are going to bed is also a bad opportunity. Find a time when both of you are available and fresh. Ask your firefighter what time of day works for them and make a date.

Take Notes: Before you get into a conversation with your spouse, or anyone else for that matter, know what you're going to talk about. Think before you speak, and get to the core of the issue. Too often, people are off-the-cuff and just speak from a surface level. They never really touch on the real issue in order to fix the problem.

Before you have a meeting of the minds, have a clear agenda of what you want to discuss. *Stay on topic.* This is not the time to go off in a hundred different directions to discuss a million little irritations—in fact, there is never a good time to do that, because you won't solve anything; you'll both just get mad.

I believe it's productive to come to the conversation with a solution as well. Think in advance of how you want this conversation to go, and then let your spouse know how you'd like to resolve the issue ... with their input too, of course.

Take the "I feel" Route of Expression: When you are communicating to your spouse about a problem, it's always smart to get off on the right foot. This is why, after years of accusatory communication with my husband, I had to learn not to begin any of our conversations with "you." Phrases like, "you are to blame; you did this; it's your fault" are not going to get you anywhere.

Instead I tell him how "I" feel. Something like, "I feel really hurt and out of the loop when you don't run things by me first. And I feel we need to work on this." The *things* might be decisions, purchases, vacations ideas ... you get the idea.

Practice Being a Good Listener: It was a big revelation for me that I was not the best listener when my husband and I were arguing. I became embarrassingly aware that I developed a 'guarded' mechanism: I would start to talk louder than him, as if trying to overpower the argument. Not listening to each other, however, just puts up barriers.

There is an old saying that we are given two ears and one mouth for a reason. I would say that listening is the most important part of good communication. It leads to awareness and keeps the temperature of the conversation comfortable.

Sharpening my skills to become a better listener has taken practice, but now my husband is less frustrated and our relationship has improved as a result.

Learn to De-Stress Beforehand: When we're feeling emotional, it's tempting to just blurt things out. Science tells us that when anger is triggered it's the amygdala (the part of the brain that deals with fear and emotions) that takes precedence over the cortex (the part that deals with common sense, good judgment, and rational thinking). This is where the old saying, "He has lost his mind," comes from.

President Thomas Jefferson once said to count to ten when you're mad and, if you are really angry, count to one hundred! Good advice.

If my husband wants an answer to something immediately and it's something that bothers me or doesn't sit right, I tell him that I'll get back to him. I know that I need to take the time to think about it. Delay keeps emotions and arguments at bay.

Start and End with the Positives: When you are about to have *that* conversation with your partner (or anyone else) it's time to build a "positivity sandwich." I learned of this communication technique back in the day when I used to teach parenting classes. Although this simple technique's name has been repackaged many times over the decades, the simple *modus operandi* remains the same.

Here's how it works. When you begin your uncomfortable conversation, bring up something positive about the other person before you dig into the meat and potatoes of the issue. Once you address the primary issue and provide some constructive criticism, you then end the conversation with something positive again. Here is an example:

(Positive) "Hon, you've become such a great communicator. I think it's one of your best traits."

(Constructive Criticism) "I've noticed lately, though, when you get home from work you are using language that I find to be shame-based. It makes me feel super-defensive with you. I understand that you're tired and probably need some time to chill when you get home, so if there is something you want to discuss with me, please don't do it when you walk through the door.

"If you'd like to talk about something that involves me, let's pick a time that suits us both. Honestly, if you approach me in a much more respectful and cheerful way, you will get my attention; it will be easier for me to listen to what you have to say and work on changes."

(Positive) "Overall this is a pretty easy fix. I appreciate you listening to me. We make a great team and are only getting better."

Bringing up constructive criticism is never easy. If you're like me, there's the worry that the person we need to address will take offense. However, this usually only occurs when we use confrontational language that blames someone right off the bat.

When you use the sandwich technique, you're essentially taking the art of conversation even further. It's thoughtful, considers the other person's feelings, and keeps everyone's dignity intact. Life is about learning our lessons so that when we are invited to grow, it's because people see our potential and inherent good. Confrontation does the exact opposite.

The Best Form of Communication Is Assertive Communication

A couple of years ago I gave a talk on assertive communication at a women's breakfast meeting. When I was done, several women, and I mean *several*, came up to me for more information about how to be assertive without feeling guilty.

I have found that learning to say "no" and being direct without feeling guilty is definitely a hot topic for women. More often than not, women in North America have grown up with the message that being nice and agreeable are the ways they should behave.

I think assertive communication is a life skill that needs to be taught to all people, beginning as early as Kindergarten. I honestly believe that if everyone learned how to communicate assertively, there would be less gossip and fewer misunderstandings. Furthermore, learning assertiveness skills leads to reduced stress, since it gives a person more confidence and a stronger self-esteem.

Assertive communication is simply a matter of saying what you mean and meaning what you say. Being assertive also means that people know where you stand and where they stand with you. Assertive communication is not rude: it's about being clear and kind. You are just letting people know how *you feel* about something.

Here are some examples of how kind, assertive communication might sound:

"Hey, let's make it for another time. I really need the day to myself, since we've been so busy lately. But I would love to take a rain check for another day."

"Can I get back to you on that? I've got to check my calendar (or confer with my partner)."

"You are very thoughtful for thinking of me but, to be honest, I'm not really a skiing kind of girl. If you're ever up for a walk, I'd love to do that with you!"

"With my dad not well at the moment, my time is really tight to be spontaneous. How about we plan something in advance, and I'll put it in my calendar?"

Setting Clear Boundaries in Your Life and Your Relationship

Firefighters have a way of allowing their siblings on the force access to their entire lives. Unfortunately, in a relationship, that can be detrimental, and at times, unacceptable. Give them an inch and they will absolutely take a mile or more. Firefighters are so dependent on one another in an emergency that they see no problem giving others *carte blanche* to all areas of their life.

For example, when we were doing house renovations, my husband gave a key to his firefighter friends who were working on our house. Can you imagine? One morning, I woke up at 5:00 a.m. on a day when Tom was at work to see one of his firefighters dry walling in our home. His wife had just had a baby, so this was a convenient time for him. Seriously?

Another wife had a firefighter slip into her basement unannounced to pick up a power washer he had lent her husband—all approved by her firefighter without her knowledge.

"Sure," her hubby had said, "just go over to the house; we keep the key under the mat."

While setting firm and clear boundaries around my life and fire marriage is no longer a problem for me, you might get blindsided from time to time by the open firefighter culture and be at a loss for what to do. Learning how to set boundaries will help you and your fire partner find a balance.

Boundaries and the Family Fence

Last summer, my husband and I put up a brand-new fence where our property borders two others. The very nice neighbour who bordered the back of our property asked my husband if he could tear down the old part of the fence, which we couldn't see behind the cedar trees that separated our two properties. True to my husband's nature, he said, "Yeah, sure; do what you want," without consulting me or getting any further details.

When I went out to water our flowers about two weeks later, I noticed a one-foot gap between our two properties where the old fence had been torn down. I wasn't comfortable with the gap between our homes, so I wrote a very nice note with my contact information and asked for the owner of the house to get back to me.

Rather than phone or email me as I asked him to do, the neighbour popped in at two very inconvenient times over the course of the day—once while I was getting ready to go to out for lunch, and the second time while I was trying to cook dinner as my husband and son watched a movie.

I'm the type of person who would rather converse by email so that I can look at details, think about things, and then make a decision. When this neighbour showed up for a second time, my husband (who trotted out his habit of being easygoing) made a deal with the guy that my son would build a slab of fence to cover the area. Once again, he did all this without discussing any of it with me or our son.

Because my husband didn't deal with the details in the beginning, he ended up creating a make-work project for our family during a difficult time when my dad wasn't well.

The fence was symbolic of the boundary problem that remained in our marriage: my husband's complete lack of boundaries, my need for them, and the fact that he wasn't respecting that need. It was time for us to seriously address our boundaries issue.

Boundary lines are essential to your sanity and peace of mind. They are needed within the confines of a relationship and for life in general.

Determine What Boundaries are Being Crossed: Take the time to identify the important boundaries and how they are being either respected or crossed.

Know That You Have a Right to Set Boundaries: You are not being selfish or a bitch. You are being sane and nipping something in the bud before it builds up and you get angry.

Make Declarations to Describe Your New Boundary: Write it down if you need to, and look at it often. Keep it short and sweet. For instance, my declaration concerning our neighbour could be, "With our family's schedule, dropping in doesn't really work with us. Here, let me give you our email again. This way, anytime we need to communicate I can forward it on to my husband, and we can answer any questions sooner rather than later." Obviously, I also had to tell hubs not to make decisions that affect our family without consulting me.

Offer Options to the Other Person: Look for win-win situations by taking control. For example, "I know that you would like to speak with me, but right now I'm in the middle of something and in a hurry. Could you please email me, and I'll get back to you in a day or so?"

Basically, you are saying, "This is what does not work for me and this is what will work for me." You can also buy yourself time, if you feel pressured. "I'm sorry; I'm just in a hurry right now and need some time to think about this. I'll have to get back to you tomorrow or the next day. I appreciate your understanding." If there is push-back, simply repeat what you've said.

Communicate Peacefully With the Other Person: I used to feel nervous speaking to people with particularly aggressive or diva personalities. But, with practice, I've learned to stay calm and even-keeled. Be clear about what you say, and give the person options if need be, *but only if they work for you.* Keep in mind that you are saying "no" to something that you are not comfortable with; you are saying "no" to a request that takes up your time or takes away your peace of mind.

Please remember that it all takes practice, so go easy on yourself. I have always found that if we've been people pleasers, the issue is in the awkwardness of the moment when people aren't used to you setting boundaries, or perhaps in feeling intimidated by a stronger personality. These are all lessons in having self-respect. Over time and with age, it will all become easy for you.

Now that you are practising assertive communication, think about areas in your life that need boundaries. Practice what you will say. When someone catches you off-guard, don't forget that you can always get back to them. Remind them that you may need to check the calendar or communicate with your spouse.

When you set limits with people, not everyone will be pleased. However, you can't really enjoy your life when boundaries are being crossed. The stress it causes will take a toll on your health. People who are respectful of you will be mature about you setting boundaries and appreciate knowing where you stand. If some people don't like them, well, that tells me a lot about who they are. When people are that self-centered, they only think of themselves and their needs.

Finding a Good Counselor

Sometimes you will go through periods in your relationship when you and your partner aren't that fond of each other—but that doesn't spell the end. A good counselor can guide you to work through those difficult periods, and show you how to rebuild. Just as in every profession, however, some counselors are better than others.

For instance, I once went to an information night with a bunch of fire wives to talk about what family counseling we had available to us when we, our partners, or our children needed help. I really looked forward to this night. But then, the professional counselor who was talking to us said something so shallow and ignorant that my blood began to boil.

Here we were, a room of vulnerable women looking for hope when we were going through some sort of marital issue with our fire partners, and he said, "If you can't find one thing you like about your spouse, then you are likely to get divorced."

He then threw on a video of another well-known motivational speaker for us to watch and that was it. I couldn't believe he was getting paid to give us this thoughtless and unhelpful advice.

I looked around the room at all of these wives who were in a tough place with their spouses, and probably not all that fond of them at that moment. Despite that, they had gotten up the courage and left their responsibilities at home to come looking for someone who could instruct them on how to keep their marriages together. They looked defeated at these hardly-uplifting words. Words either build or tear down, and these words built absolutely nothing.

To save these women from despair, I piped up after the video and put my heart out there. At the time, I was remembering when we'd had our first child, and I was annoyed because I felt like a cow: just a body that everyone wanted. I said, "There are times you don't like your spouse, like maybe after you have a baby and he wants sex and your baby needs your boobs. And sometimes when you are going through a hard time, you may not like anything about them at that moment. But here's the thing. You fell in love with them once, and you will fall in love again. You just need to know the phases that all marriages go through, and what's possible when you make it over the hurdles."

The women I sat with looked at me with a sense of relief.

Not everyone has the "gift" to counsel. If you aren't comfortable with a counselor, try someone else. Do your research, or ask some of your friends that have had counselling, who they might recommend.

Good counselors are skilled at getting people to talk, and trained to help you come up with great solutions. They know the right questions to ask, and they interject when necessary to guide you in self-reflection and put things into perspective.

A good counselor makes you feel at ease, and never crosses any personal lines with you by being unprofessionally friendly. I remember when a friend of mine went to couples' therapy, and the counselor did some complaining about her own ex-husband. She also asked my friend for advice about her kids! Can you believe it? That was absolutely crossing a line.

Good counseling motivates you to become better, and helps you to understand that the *power* to change is in your hands. It does not endorse blaming, scapegoating, or creating enemies with other people. It is instead designed to teach you how to set boundaries and communicate so that you will no longer feel the need to blame others.

Good counseling is supportive, asks you what your intentions are and directs you to set goals. My own counselor made it clear that her methods were solution-based, and included giving me homework to complete each week. She also let me know when I "graduated" and no longer had to receive further counseling. That is a good counselor. Keeping you on the payroll just to come in and complain every week without regular solutions is not good therapy.

I came to love marriage counseling, especially for my husband's sake. Not many firefighters have someone, besides you, to open up and talk to. But also, it's really healthy to have an objective third party in the room to keep you both on topic, steer you in the right direction, and then give you something to practice.

Where there used to be a negative stigma attached to counseling in some fire halls, or just in general, I have personally witnessed a real turnaround. I see more and more men talking openly about their counseling experiences and encouraging their brothers to partake when they are going through emotional rough patches.

For me, attending a counseling session is also like taking a marriage refresher course: it helps Tom and me learn the tools necessary to make our marriage work.

If, by chance, your insurance does not cover counseling and it's too much to pay, find a support group, a church program, some online courses, or even some DVDs the two of you can use. Sometimes you can even hire a qualified counselor who can facilitate you and your partner in a group setting, where they charge less.

I used to have my doubts about counseling, and so did my husband, but it has been a valuable tool in working through the challenges in our marriage.

Taking a Trip Down Memory Lane

One way to stay committed to your relationship when the going gets tough is to look back and remember all the things that you loved about your partner in the beginning. It may feel hard sometimes, but I truly think that stepping back to remember what the two of you once were is a reminder of what lies underneath all the bitterness.

When you take a moment to reflect on some of these questions, you focus on the positive. Share them with your partner. It will make you both feel better hearing these questions answered by each other.

1) What qualities in your partner-to-be did you love when you first met them?
2) What attracted you to them in the first place?
3) What made you decide that they were the one for you?
4) How can taking a trip down memory lane re-inspire you to stay the course in your marriage?

Sometimes doing something together without a group of friends (or the kids) will rekindle your feelings for each other and remind you why you first got together. When life gets in the way, make a date, and make time for one another.

For today, choose to remember only the good qualities in your partner before the busyness of life got in the way.

Vive La Difference

One of my favorite plays, *Mom's the Word*, had me roaring with laughter in the interactions between a husband and his wife. And although I can't remember it verbatim, I remember one scene in which the husband comes into the kitchen, as he usually does, to open the refrigerator door.

His wife sits there, watching her husband as he looks for something, and the audience hears her internal dialogue: "Alright, he's coming into the kitchen, he's opened the refrigerator door, and he's going to ask me where something is."

Sure enough he asks, "Where's the mayonnaise?"

Suddenly, angel harmonies play in the background. While the rest of the refrigerator remains dark, a celestial glow hovers over a jar of mayonnaise sitting, guess where? Right smack in front of his face.

His wife, as usual, spots the mayo, gets up from where she's just sat down with a book for her five minutes of peace, and shows him where the mayo is.

The play originated in Canada, and although it is now considered an international success, the humor in moments such as this may not translate across the Atlantic, particularly in France. You see, French women know something that some North American women still do not: men are not women and women are not men. Hence, *"Vive La Difference,"* a phrase often used to refer to the sexes and, when translated, simply means, "long live the difference!"

In 1992, John Gray wrote the ground-breaking book, *Men are from Mars, Women are from Venus*, which highlights the innate differences between men and women. This is in contrast to the theory that boys take on masculine traits and girls take on feminine traits through socialization and society's expectations of them.

While society does play its part in putting pressure on men to be tough and women to be perfect, there are certainly vast psychological and biological differences between the sexes, a reality that cannot be denied.

Here are a few more notable differences, according to John Gray as well as authors of *Men are Like Waffles, Women are Like Spaghetti*, Bill and Pam Farrel:

Women see more of what's going on around them than men, because men don't have the peripheral vision that we do.

Women have a better sense of smell than men.

Men don't process higher pitched voices easily, so they automatically tune them out. If you want the men in your life to hear you, lower your voice a little and talk less. It's science, my friend.

Women want to solve issues immediately, whereas men can compartmentalize them. This is why, even if there is a pressing problem, with their intense ability to focus, men are able to deal with it *after* they watch the football game! Women, on the other hand, can't stop thinking about something until it is solved.

In my experience, guys seem to be gifted when it comes to left-brained tasks such as reading instructions and putting stuff together (let's not confuse that with directions, however). Although it's not my forte, if I had to, I'm sure I could set these things up myself. Come to think of it, no, I wouldn't; I'd probably hire someone.

I've also found that men and women remember details differently, too, such as when my husband came home with news one day:

My husband: "Hey, hon, my friend and his wife had a baby!"

Me: "That's so exciting. What did they have?"

My husband: "I don't know."

Me: "What do you mean, you don't know?"

My husband: "I didn't ask."

Me: "Well, where was the baby born, then?"

My husband: "I'm not sure."

He remembered what he saw as the important details: that his friend was happy with a healthy new baby.

In her book, *What French Women Know: About Love, Sex, and Other Matters of the Heart and Mind*, American author Debra Ollivier talks about a mixed dinner party she attended in France. There, the French women did not participate in the familiar "bitch session … or battle of the sexes with the men." In fact, "In France, men and women actually like one another a lot and they enjoy their mutual company. They spar, they debate. They flirt."

In France, men and women love their differences, and it leaves room for more enjoyment in their relationships. There is no expectation that men should act like women or vice versa. As Debra Ollivier said, "You can take a $500 lifestyle workshop in America to get wind of this, or you can have a drink with a French woman." Save your money and go for the cocktail.

Tom's Corner

The point of acknowledging the differences between you and your partner is not just to create understanding, but also to put yourself in a better position to prevent further irritation.

For instance, to solve the problem of my husband not being able to "spot the mayonnaise" in the refrigerator, and to save myself from the endless questions of where his favorite condiments were, I created "Tom's Corner" in our refrigerator door rack. I took note of all the things my hubby repeatedly asked me for, like his favorite hot sauce, salad dressing, and soya sauce, and put them into one nice, tidy section. He now has no problem finding his favorite things. He even has his own little salt and pepper in there. I'm happy, he's happy. It's a win-win.

Connection Tools

Going Away Just the Two of You

For the longest time I couldn't put my finger on it. While both Tom and I connected in so many ways as a couple, there was something missing in our marriage, something I envied unwittingly in others, but I couldn't figure out.

Then it dawned on me, and I was actually embarrassed.

With the exception of us spending one week alone on our honeymoon, the two of us had never been away on vacation together, just the two of us. All of our vacations were either spent sharing the family cabin with his parents, a sibling or two, and their family, or going away with friends. The vacation schedule was never our own.

In fact, on the second week of our honeymoon, we invited a bunch of friends and their kids to the cabin because that's what we'd always done. Before we knew it, our little love nest turned into Camp Howdy. Instead of making fresh bread and romantic dinners each night, our kitchen transformed into a cafeteria of mass food production: chicken fingers, hot dogs, and vats of home-made chilli. All delicious, of course, just not on my honeymoon.

For that first glorious week, however, my husband and I did make fresh bread every morning with our brand-new bread maker (a wedding gift from my girlfriends), slept in front of a beautiful fire each night, and took the boat across the lake for a romantic dinner at the Okanagan Resort. My husband had made breakfast every morning, one of which included a stack of heart-shaped pancakes.

Looking back now, I cannot believe we invited people on our honeymoon—it makes me wince. It was the first marriage mistake we made, starting out. Unfortunately, it took a couple of decades for us to figure out that going away together, just the two of us, was one of the most important things we could do to connect.

But I guess it's better late than never, right?

Fast forward twenty-three years, and Tom and I took our first married vacation together for seven splendid, uninterrupt-ed days on a road trip to Washington State. We spent a foodie's dream night in Seattle, then drove to the Gorge, a breathtaking, outdoor concert venue just outside of wine country's Wenatchee to see Dave Matthews, a fantastic American musician.

For one whole week, the two of us enjoyed romantic walks along the Columbia River, trips to the farmers' market, and an afternoon in the charming German-styled town of Leavenworth. There, we drank beer and ate delicious sausages at the year-round beer garden in the town square. We enjoyed a succulent dinner of the best German-style food of our lives (enormous platter fondue) at the very popular Mozart's Restaurant. Then, because we had no timeline, Tom and I were free to be spontaneous and explore.

On one of our excursions, we spotted a street called Love Lane and decided to follow it. What we found down the narrow, windy dirt road was a charming, 1917 bed and breakfast called Warm Springs. A welcome sign greeted us to "come on in and try our wines." For almost two hours, we sat at the wine-tasting bar while the owner regaled us with his wit and we enjoyed a stunning view of the rushing Columbia River.

En route home, we found ourselves barely moving through the concert traffic, so we decided to pull over and booked into the friendly, family-run Alpine Rivers Inn for another two days. Had we not been alone, we probably wouldn't have been able to enjoy more time together in these spur-of-the-moment adventures.

When we returned home the following week, it wasn't until I saw my therapist that I could tell her I had figured out what we had been missing. Talk about a simple fix.

When you belong to a fire family, it is no doubt tempting to do a lot of things together, and that includes going away on vacations in a group. As well, because firefighters and their wives usually share the same trait of independence, we can forget how important it is to get out of town just to be together and reconnect. When we do this, we invite ourselves back into the honeymoon stage of our lives, allowing us to remember all the reasons why we like each other.

Remember, You Are on the Same Team

There was a fire couple I knew who were always competing with each other: true rivals. They'd compete over who was the better parent, who had the better job, and, in the kitchen, who had the better way of cutting and preparation.

Dragging childish rivalry into your relationship does not make for a good one and, honestly, I could never understand the whole spouse-competition thing. I mean, aren't we on the same team? Don't we share a vision? Aren't we going down the same road together?

Competing against each other while on the same team breeds disconnection and discontent. If we think about it, there isn't a sports team in the world that would win if they had opponents on the same team. When you're on a winning team, you utilize each other's talents by working off of them. You are not against each other, you are for each other.

While I've not been competitive with my husband, I did feel I was often at odds with the way he would speak to our children when it came to discipline. I felt that we should always take a gentler approach that involved more explanation; in the back of my mind, I felt that their self-esteem would be tarnished otherwise.

Then I remembered some great wisdom I heard about raising children with your spouse. You have got to stand back and let your partner raise them, too. As long as it's healthy discipline and not corporal (which is horrific), a child's self-esteem benefits from a combination of parenting methods, whether that is a gradual and encouraging approach, a no-nonsense, nip-it-in-the-bud attitude, or anything in between.

While I must give myself some credit for not being a wimpy mom in the discipline department, my husband's approach was different from mine, and our kids benefitted from both of our influences. I had to remember that, in our own special ways, we each brought a lot of character-building, teachable moments to our children. We contributed our unique personalities to the raising of our boys.

Trusting my husband to be a father to our kids was a good lesson for me; otherwise, our boys might not have turned out with the grit they need to handle criticism and failure.

Focusing on what both you and your partner bring to the table in your relationship is what successful teams do. One poem that I've heard read at countless weddings is 1 Corinthians 13:4-7:

Love is patient, love is kind.
It does not envy, it does not boast, it is not proud.
It does not dishonor others, it is not self-seeking,
it is not easily angered, it keeps no record of wrongs.
Love does not delight in evil but rejoices with the truth.
It always protects, always trusts, always hopes,
always perseveres.

Translation: You're on the same team.

Women and Men and Sex

I was trying to think of what angle to take when discussing sex in this book because, of course, sex is such a personal thing. Even in my group of girlfriends, we don't discuss it because it's so private. It's also a complex subject. To have a good sex life with your partner, it needs to feel fulfilling, safe, pleasurable, and also healthy.

Another thing to remember, just like the phases of a relationship, is that the sex life you and your partner share will also go through phases. Your sex life will evolve over the course of your relationship, particularly after you have babies, feel exhausted with life, and when there are hormone issues on either side. Operations and health problems may mean that you have sex less frequently than you used to.

I see this as an opportunity to develop intimacy in other ways: spending time talking, holding hands while watching a movie, going for walks, and expressing love and gratitude to your partner.

Moreover, if there are issues of erectile dysfunction or low libido (both come with age, stress, and hormone issues), a trip to the doctor to get additional assistance is beneficial. Don't feel embarrassed or fearful. These are just normal phases that all couples go through, and you've got decades of a healthy sex life ahead of you.

When I had some fire wives over for brunch, the one thing they all agreed on when it came to sex was that it must be made a priority. As one of my friends said, "My husband and I've been together since we were teenagers, so if we didn't make it a priority, we'd just be pals. It's also the one thing that reminds us that we are truly a husband and wife."

For me, if my husband and I go without it for too long, we both get cranky; so yes, sex is a great release, and I always feel reconnected and adored when my husband and I make sex an important part of our marriage.

But while making sex a priority keeps you connected, being unhappy with your sex life will do just the opposite. Since I am not a sex therapist and there is nothing you don't already know about sex, I don't feel qualified to speak on most specific issues. However, I would like to briefly look at something I have been finding personally disturbing lately: some people's extremely unhealthy addiction to porn and what it will do to a relationship.

I'm not against visual stimulation, and I've enjoyed watching soft porn with my husband; I feel there is nothing wrong with mutual enjoyment. However, our culture has become extreme in this department, to the point where expectations can become very unrealistic and partners can feel inadequate.

When any kind of porn begins to interfere with your relationship, then you know that it's unhealthy and needs to be dealt with. In addition to opening up the lines of communication, counseling might be key to helping you both. Whenever there are problems with intimacy, there are usually unresolved blocks that are keeping a person from developing healthy relationships.

Sometimes, good sex takes some planning as the years proceed and you've been together for a while.

With many women, foreplay begins hours before she gets into bed with her partner; feeling sensuous and excited for sex begins in a woman's brain. So, before you get to the main event, thinking about it long beforehand and preparing for it will get you in the mood.

Also, take a look at your bedroom to see if it needs a little makeover. De-cluttering is always a good idea. It's easy for bedrooms to become places where we throw the laundry, let the crosswords and maybe the wine glasses pile up! However, clutter in any room will zap your energy. Transforming your bedroom into a boudoir is a good start. Do you need new sheets? Some beautiful pillows? Gorgeous, inspiring pictures?

How about your bathroom? If you like to take a warm, sensuous bath before bed, you can add a few extras: some fragrant oil, bath salts, or an exfoliant. How about some music to listen to, or a drink that sits on the side of your bath? Perhaps some big, fluffy towels, or lotion so that you can get a foot rub in too!

How's the lingerie drawer? Do you have something comfortable but sexy to slip into? Don't forget the bedside table. Does it have a few toys and magic potions on hand to turn up the heat? Of course, if you have little kids, you don't want them finding something only to use it as a microphone, so do keep things private.

Just like the road trip my husband and I took, sometimes all it takes is just a few simple changes to turn a lot of things around.

Internal Tools

The Golden Rule

Treat others the way you'd like to be treated.

Imagine how many relationships would stay together if the Golden Rule were practiced consistently. Do unto others as you would have done unto you. I know a lot of couples would say, "Yeah, but they need to be nice to me first." But how is that going to work if you are both waiting for the other?

The Golden Rule is actually an unchangeable universal principle. This Tool is simply about being thoughtful, considerate, and all in all decent human beings towards each other, which in turn brings out the best in everyone. It doesn't cost a penny to practice these good deeds, but they do pay out great dividends. In fact, I think that if everyone practiced the Golden Rule in all their relationships, everyone would get along.

Practising the Golden Rule is possibly the number-one relationship secret, and it's pretty basic. Here are some Golden Rule practices that will make all of your relationships better.

Saying Sorry

Saying you are sorry or admitting to being wrong is very disarming. The egos drop and defenses go down, just with these two very powerful words. If you are wrong about something, have taken an argument too far, or just said something not nice, simply say you are sorry. It doesn't make you weak; instead, it will bring the two of you closer together.

If you are not an apologizer, learn to become one. Nothing is worse than a superior personality who claims to always be right. It's okay to be wrong; you're only human, and we all make mistakes.

Generosity

According to an article written by Tara Parker-Pope in *The New York Times Magazine* (printed December 11, 2011), researchers from the University of Virginia's National Marriage Project found by studying 2,087 married men and women that spouses who were generous and kind towards one another had very happy marriages. Those couples who did not do kind things for their partner were not all that happy.

While the simple act of being generous to your partner lacks the hard-core "boot camp" strategy some couples are looking for to fix their relationships, the power of generosity cannot be overstated.

It has been said that relationships are not a fifty-fifty proposition, but rather a one hundred-one hundred proposition. Creating the relationship you want means that you have to know your partner, but also you have to be willing to be generous of spirit with them.

For instance, one of the things I love to do for my husband is wake up and make him coffee before he goes to the fire hall. I can see how tired he is, and because I'm an early bird, it's easy for me to be generous in this department.

Generosity with your partner is simply thinking about what you can do to make their life a little nicer.

Antonyms of generosity are stinginess and meanness. Does that sound like the type of relationship that would produce happiness? It seems that the problem with our culture these days is that ego and narcissism have become epidemic. If you have too much of either, your relationship will be extremely difficult.

For instance, many years ago, a woman was complaining to me about her husband; she was irritated that he had the nerve to express his feelings about what he would like from her. He liked it when they gave each other massages; she hated it.

"Well, can't you just give each other massages once in a while?" I asked.

"Are you f*@king kidding me?" she blurted out. "I'm not doing that."

They're no longer together.

Not too long ago, a firefighter friend of ours confided that he was frustrated with his wife's lack of consideration for him when he got home from work. "She's home hours before me, and yet waits for me to come home to get the BBQ on!"

If you want a happy marriage, be generous, thoughtful, and considerate.

Expressing the Golden Principles

"Do unto others" is a boomerang.
Whatever you decide to throw out there will return to you.
If you do not like what comes back—change your output.
MERLYN GABRIEL MILLER

People Feel Loved and Respected When They are Admired: The Golden Principles here are honor and reliability. To feel loved, a person needs to feel cherished, and that their partner respects them.

As I mentioned at the beginning of this book, you are your firefighter's true best friend, and they rely on your opinion. When you honor them with compliments, praise and point out their achievements, they will feel good about themselves and count on you when they need a little boost or pep talk. And come on, let's be honest here: who better to look up to and admire more than a firefighter, the ultimate hero! Like it or not, everyone has an ego, and it needs attention.

Acknowledge Them When They Get Home: The Golden Principles here are unity, kindness, and trust. I will never forget what author Toni Morrison once said about acknowledging your children. "When they come into a room, don't criticize but let your face light up when you see them instead."

The same, of course, applies to all human beings. When you acknowledge another human being, you are saying, "I see you." Your connection creates unity and a feeling of togetherness. I can't stand people who ignore others; to me, it is the absolute height of rudeness. Acknowledging others is showing kindness.

When your firefighter gets home, and God knows what kind of a day they've had, take a minute to welcome them. If you get home after them, maybe the two of you can have a glass of wine together to catch up on each other's day so you both know where you're at. When your partner knows you'll acknowledge them when they get home, they can trust what coming home will feel like.

Confer With Them: The Golden Principles here are courtesy, consideration, and honesty. Looking back now, I cannot believe what I used to do to my husband. He has always had the good courtesy of checking in with me to see if he could go out for a beer with the guys after work, or to take a shift for another firefighter. Me ... well, I didn't confer with him very often about stuff, including not letting him know one year that I'd asked my whole family—including extended family—for Christmas dinner until the week before.

Sometimes, we keep things from our firefighters simply because we learn to handle things on our own. Either that, or we want to wait for the right time to let them know that the kids are in trouble at school, the in-laws are coming to visit or, yes, a whole side of the family is coming for dinner.

It's not always easy to find the right time when they're tired and cranky after a night shift, a day shift, or an extra shift. Here's the thing: it is better to confer with them on most things, because you would want them to do the same with you ... it's considerate.

One of the quickest ways to give your firefighter "news" is to shoot off a text or an email; then they will at least have some time to mull stuff over before they come home. Your partner just wants you to be honest and include them in what's going on at home; otherwise, they'll feel out of the loop, and that'll just cause them unnecessary stress and worry.

Accept Their Individual Need for Space: The Golden Principles here are freedom, fun, and personal fulfillment. Listen, you need a little space all your own, too. This is not a one-sided luxury, but rather a two-sided necessity. Author Virginia Woolf famously said that women "need a room of one's own." We all do.

When we take the time to relax from the day's stress in our own space, we bring those cortisol levels back into balance. It's no secret that chronic stress makes people sick. When a person gets exhausted, unbalanced cortisol levels can cause testosterone to dip, resulting in cranky or irritable moods. This is especially notable in men.

When we get to be alone to simply put our feet up and read a good book, cocoon in the basement with a remote control in hand, or just sit in the hot tub to 'Zen out,' we return restored and fulfilled. Everyone deserves a one-person party and the freedom to hang out alone.

Never Criticize, Argue, or Humiliate in Public: The Golden Principles here are self-discipline and dignity. Hopefully, you are not the sort of person who does this to your significant other. Whenever I hear a couple bicker or criticize each other in a public space, I feel my toes curl. Nothing is more demeaning than giving your partner a lecture, proving them wrong, or otherwise condemning them in front of others, and they will hate you for it.

This type of behavior also makes other people feel horribly uncomfortable and, if it is a habit, you won't be asked out again with other couples.

If you have a problem with your partner, exercise self-discipline and talk to them later in private. Not only is this the gracious way to handle things for both them and you it also keeps your partner's dignity in tact.

By the way, the same goes for dealing with children: never humiliate them in front of people. Take them to a room privately to speak to them. Waiting to embarrass or humiliate a person when there's an audience is passive-aggressive behavior, and it will do far more harm than good.

Allow Them to Speak: The Golden Principles here are harmony and peace. Once in a while, your partner will go out on a limb when the two of you are arguing to tell you how they feel, and you need to hear that.

The problem for me was when my husband went to talk, I'd get defensive. I found myself overpowering him with my words. "You never listen to me," was the complaint I *finally* heard from him when I learned to listen to what my man had to say.

Everyone deserves to be heard, but often, we will talk right over the person we're arguing with, pushing our volume higher and higher. By the end of the disagreement, we have absolutely no idea what the other person said.

One breakthrough I had in this department was when I practiced restraint and let my husband bring up stuff he wanted to change in our house. He stopped talking fifteen minutes later. I think even he was surprised.

Since I became a better listener, our marriage has become more harmonious and peaceful. And why wouldn't it? Each of us deserves to be heard when we want to air our opinions or negotiate change, even if we don't agree with each other.

Marriage Grows Us

*You don't develop courage by being happy
in your relationships every day. You develop it by surviving difficult
times and challenging adversity.*
EPICURUS

It has been said that marriage will highlight what needs to be made whole within you. Having an intimate partnership will do that! Any unresolved, negative habits or dysfunctional patterns we bring into a relationship will become a source of conflict, whether it's your first, second—even third—marriage, or if you haven't tied the knot yet. Until you solve your internal problems, you will continue to meet up with them in every relationship.

Marriage, however, is supposed to improve us; it brings to light the quirks we need to transform. For example, when we have someone in our life who does things differently than we do, we either learn how to become more flexible or let our dysfunction creep in and become a constant state of dissatisfaction.

After a disagreement, when the frustration dies down, remember to use it as an opportunity to change, communicate better, or learn more about the both of you. No relationship is more intimate, vulnerable, infuriating, or wonderful than your marriage, and there is no relationship that will make you grow into a better version of yourself.

For me personally, being married to a firefighter has made me a stronger woman. Firefighters know that they can be hard to live with; they really do. Over time and through many years of experience in your fire relationship, you'll see that the two of you will grow together. You'll actually be impressed with how your relationship has smoothed out the two of you.

71

When I was first married to my hubby, I could be very dramatic and irrational. That's youth for you. Since then, we've been through the stresses of in-law problems, becoming parents, financial struggles, the loss of people we loved deeply, health issues, and many other life adjustments.

Now that I'm in my fifties, I've learned a great many things from living life with another person. I've mellowed because, after plenty of practice, I now know that some arguments are just not worth it. I used to be very argumentative with my husband, and there were some words said I could never take back.

Today, my husband and I laugh at situations that used to set us off. I have also learned the lovely art of detachment, so now he doesn't get on my nerves like he used to!

And Last but Not Least, Who Cares about the Toothpaste!

Many years ago, a little handbook written by author Richard Carlson, PhD, came on the market. It was called *Don't Sweat the Small Stuff ... and it's all Small Stuff.* Of course, the saying has been around for years, but it certainly reminds you not to make the little things into big things. If we fret over all the little things in life, how on God's green earth will we be able to handle the really big stuff?

If you can't stand how he squeezes the toothpaste, don't sweat it. Solve the issue by ensuring you each have your very own tube. I constantly lose the caps of my toothpaste. Usually they fall on the ground and I, while chatting on the phone, subconsciously pick them up and throw them into the recycling. So, yes, I survive with toothpaste and no cap.

My husband, on the other hand, is gloriously neat and tidy with his tube. He wipes it regularly so toothpaste doesn't clump at the top, replaces the cap tightly, and puts it away into his neat and uncluttered drawer.

To me, making sure the dishes are done is important. To me, making sure I buy healthy and nutritious food for my family is important. How I squeeze my toothpaste? Not important.

Do not buy into the toilet paper wars, the toothpaste wars, or any other marital cliché for that matter. If one of you is picky and the other is not (which is usually the case) solve the issue by making things easy. Buy your own toothpaste.

CHAPTER FOUR

The Predictable Stages of a Fire Relationship

Our lives are a work in progress.
SUSAN TAYLOR

Marriage: The Hardest Relationship You'll Ever Have

My husband and I had a bad fight. On a scale from one to ten, this one registered a fifteen. But to this day, I still have no idea what it was about.

I do remember, however, that the unkind words I spoke to him haunted me. After a torturous couple days of not speaking to each other, it dawned on me that we barely spent a few seconds on the real issue at hand. Instead, we went off into a shedload of directions, screaming small hurts that had piled up over time and were swept under the rug of avoidance.

Once I had time to process what had happened between us, I remembered telling him that ours was the hardest relationship I'd ever had.

And then it hit me.

Of course this was the hardest relationship I'd ever had! He was the only person I'd had kids with, shared finances with, had in-law problems with ... Shall I go on?

The fact is, anyone who was in a relationship with you prior to the relationship you have with your long-term partner got off easy. They haven't gotten up in the middle of the night to change dirty diapers, held your hand in labor, or lived with you long enough to get bothered by your habits and housework fetishes (or lack thereof).

To say that your marriage is the hardest relationship that you'll ever have is true. The other ones were easier because they didn't have any of the committed responsibilities that come with marriage.

Rough patches aren't just in relationships—we experience them throughout life. So, whether you lose a job, can't get pregnant, have an identity crisis, or feel lonely, know that every human being will go through challenges that will test their trust, hope, and faith in life.

This chapter will look at the common rough patches in a fire relationship. My raw honesty in these matters is not meant to bring you down or make you feel negative about your relationship. It's about giving you an honest heads-up of what you can expect in your fire relationship, and knowing that it's not the end of the world.

One of the mantras I like to repeat to myself when going through a rough patch is "this too shall pass." Life is constantly changing, and as human beings we are continually being stretched in order to shape our character. The problem you're having today might very well be something you'll have a good laugh about tomorrow.

And though it might not be a time you look back on and remember fondly, you will have garnered some very important insight into your life. Keep in mind Tony Robbins's aphorism, "Things don't happen to you; they happen for you."

This Too Shall Pass

When you've had a fight with your spouse,
this too shall pass.
When you go to the bank and see nothing left,
this too shall pass.
When you get fired from your job,
this too shall pass.
When you send drunk, nasty emails to a frenemy,
this too shall pass.
Look at whatever problem you're facing today and remember,
This too shall pass.

The Baggage We Bring to Relationships

My parents separated when I was four and divorced when I was nine. My sister and I spent our lives in the full love and custody of our mother, but we rarely saw our father. In addition, all of my maternal extended family members—aunts and uncles—have been married twice or more.

With this experience of multiple marriages, I have rarely witnessed couples working it out to stay together through thick and thin. So, while most of them are now in long-term and happy second marriages, the truth was I was still at a loss for role models.

Believing that my husband and I would divorce every time we had a problem was the "baggage" I brought into my relationship with him. Baggage, of course, is a combination of all the weird habits and beliefs we carry with us simply from experiencing all that we have in life. In my case, my baggage was a bunch of divorced relatives and how they handled conflict.

The interesting thing, though, is that while this is what we come to learn, it by no means needs to be a truthful way to live our lives. For every marriage that ended in divorce in my extended family, there are hundreds more marriages that have lasted the test of time and are happy.

Regardless of your role models and whether they were good or bad, you are influenced by them. However, you don't have to repeat the family cycle. Look instead to people whom you admire, and then begin structuring your ideal relationship accordingly.

The Seven-Year and Twenty-Year Itch

Long before I even thought about settling down, I worked with a beautiful human being, Joanne, who became a tremendous friend of mine. She gave me some wise advice about the predictable stages of a marriage. She told me that all couples, especially when they're in the season of parenting young children, go through challenging times, and may even think their relationship is over.

"But hold on and be patient," she said, "because the two of you will come back together again."

Now when I hear of a fire couple who have children and have decided to separate, I'm never surprised to hear that the kids are about seven years of age and under. I mean, let's be honest; as much as we love our children, they're all-consuming. And it results in couples who either don't get enough time or don't make enough time to nurture their relationship. But Joanne's advice would always stay with me, especially when my husband and I had little kids, and I want you to remember this, too.

The second period when couples can start to think about separating is around the "married for twenty years" mark (give or take a few). That's usually when the kids have grown up, are going off to college, or are moving out. If two people in a relationship have put all of their attention into the kids, or have spent too much time with their buddies at the fire department, their relationship has gone unnurtured for too long. Couples may then look at one another as strangers and be eager to move on.

By the way, this is also the classic time when mid-life crises occur.

Some Interesting Facts About Relationships

All Relationships Go Through Stages That Aren't That Great. Just as we can predict the cycle of nature's four seasons from spring through winter, relationships too are cyclical. At the beginning of any relationship (the spring and summer times), you feel enamored and romantically excited by your new relationship.

There are also the more sobering seasons of your relationship when the effects of fall and winter come into play. Winter is the toughest season of a relationship, and it feels cold and desolate.

It's Human, My Dear, to Want to Give up Sometimes. Many relationships, especially the happiest ones, have been through enough rough patches to have entertained the idea of ending their partnership at one point or another. Going through a rough patch is grueling and feels at times like it would be easier to throw in the towel than go beyond the pain of working it out.

However, those couples who work through things together, even when they've never felt further apart, will reap the rewards later when they become a truly solid couple admired by others—a couple that people could never in a million years have guessed that they'd been to hell and back ... but they have.

Expect at Least Ten Years of Irreconcilable Differences. I heard a marriage therapist on television say that out of a thirty-year marriage, a couple can expect to experience at least ten years of irreconcilable differences. When I heard that, it floored me; but it also made me feel a little better about my marriage and the normal rough patches my husband and I go through.

There are Benefits to Sticking It Out. Here's something else I want you to remember—when you and your partner make the effort to work through things and stick out the tough times, you can expect to be even more connected as a couple just a few years down the road.

You are Normal. By the way, are you aware that throughout their relationship, couples fall in and out of love several times? So, yes, you are normal.

The Predictable Growing Pains of Relationships

If there is one thing no one ever told me—including the two marriage counselors my husband and I saw—it is that all relationships go through very predictable stages. Knowing what these stages are enlightened me, and I think it will really benefit you, too.

Here they are. For the most part, they go in order; however, there are always exceptions to the rule.

The Celebratory Stage

The Disillusionment Stage

The Big Choices Stage

The Bridge Stage

The New Skills Stage

The Evolution Stage

The Juicy Peach Stage

The Celebratory Stage

This is the exciting stage, when you are still a new couple and you just love all those unique quirks about your partner: the way they eat, walk, talk, and laugh.

This stage is the romantic one, when you will do anything for each other: cook dinner, bring gifts, give out compliments, and wear sexy lingerie. You feel giddy, and you can't stop thinking about one another when you are apart, or wait to see them when they get home.

This is also a really fulfilling time for romance and regular sex. You look forward to a great future and share exciting dreams together. Enjoy it while you can, because the next stage is ...

The Disillusionment Stage

Remember all those cute little "quirks" you loved about your significant other when you first met? Well, they just aren't that cute anymore. Yes, you still love your partner, but get ready for the battle of the wills to emerge—especially if you start having children or are sharing children with an ex-partner. It's also around this time that in-law issues begin to emerge—the honeymoon period might be over with them, too!

Stress may enter your relationship now as you and your partner battle over family traditions and decisions around where you will spend the special holidays ... with yours or theirs. Naturally, it depends on who your in-laws are, and they could be flexible and lovely.

You also get more glimpses of your partner in those hardly-romantic moments, say, sitting on the toilet with the door wide open. This is also the time when the reality of shared expenses and the lack of money come into play, since you now have more bills to pay, and possibly a mortgage or support payments.

You may also begin to experience some resentment during this stage, and be upset at your firefighter for barely being home. When you fight, you can say mean things, and feelings will be hurt. This stage is when a lot of couples give up, because it's *the toughest part of the climb*. Unfortunately, not everyone chooses to work through the disillusionment stage and, sadly, this is when most divorces occur.

Just so you know, the disillusionment stage doesn't necessarily have a time limit on it, either. It could last a few short years or several long ones, depending on how quickly you get help for your problems.

When Your Marriage Hits Bottom: I remember a time when my husband and I had hit bottom as partners—simply, I believe, because the two of us were emotionally wrecked. We'd been through a very trying four years, where we experienced just about every life stress imaginable.

The hardest part for me, however, was when my husband began medical treatment for his arthritis and his personality began to change. He became increasingly moody. The words he would speak to the kids and me became critical and, at times, callous. We did not realize how his medication would affect him. I tried talking to him about it, but he was in complete denial that he'd changed and adamant to continue treatment.

On the one hand, I understood his desperation to continue his medications: he had been through the horror of a near-zero white blood cell count and a period of reactive arthritis so severe that he had to be admitted to a rehabilitation facility in order to learn how to walk properly again. On the other hand, if he was going to continue using these medications, he'd have to learn to manage his frustration.

It wasn't until both our little boys came to me upset about the change in their dad that I had to grow a rock-solid backbone and confront him. He came home one morning and like clockwork began to lace into me for some minor household infraction. I snapped. I told him how he was affecting our family, especially our sons.

Not believing a word I said, he sat at the kitchen table. Focused completely on the newspaper, he said with a smirk, "I'm not affecting the kids."

With that, an anger ascended in me that I'd never felt with him. To this day, I cannot remember how I got downstairs to retrieve our kids.

"Get upstairs now, you two, and you tell your dad what he is doing to you!"

"Okay, Mom," they said. Wide-eyed and surprised, they quickly complied. Our boys returned to where Tom was still reading his newspaper.

"Now you kids say to Dad everything you've been telling me about what you've been feeling. Don't hold anything back."

As my husband heard what the kids thought, he realized the truth about how he was affecting his children. He was devastated.

Barely able to speak, he begged our boys for forgiveness and apologized to them for how he'd been treating us all. Finally, after months of holding in a great deal of emotional pain, my man broke down.

He then picked up the phone and, still sobbing, called our marriage counselor. Sensing the desperation in his voice, the counselor arrived at our home only a couple of hours later. My husband's break*down* was our family's break*through*.

The Winter Season of a Relationship:

We went through fire and water, but you brought us
to a place of abundance.
PSALM 66:12

Winter is truly the worst season of a relationship. You're despondent, and maybe a little frightened and angry, because your relationship feels hopeless. Maybe it's a serious health issue, depression, a job loss, or financial problems. Whatever it is, it has hurt your relationship seemingly beyond repair.

The emotional distance between you is deep and one or both of you feel done. Who, you wonder, is this stranger I'm looking at? This is the time in a relationship when you experience feelings of anguish and loss.

It was my husband's and my winter period when his personality had changed so much. I was ready to walk away from my marriage. I couldn't imagine going through this pain any longer. Something had to change, or it was going to be over.

More than half of all firefighter marriages don't make it through the winter period, and for a number of reasons.

However, like the great expeditions of years past, the only ones who survive the winter's cold muster up that one shred of hope, hold on for dear life, and lean into the support of good friends, family, and faith to make it through.

Logically, I knew that there was too much to lose if we threw it all away, so I took pause. Being a child of divorce, I knew that breaking up a family was never an easy solution. And though I'd never personally witnessed anyone working through the rough patches of marriage, I learned in my research for this book that coming back from the winter season of a relationship is certainly possible.

As I have mentioned, you need to practice foresight, and imagine what life might be like without each other if you decide to end your relationship.

As I look back now over what my husband and I endured, I can't believe that we made it through. But thank God we did. Keep in mind that even if you and your partner are in the season of winter, spring is just around the corner. The seeds of flowers that you can't yet see under the earth's frozen surface will bloom again.

When Trust Is Broken: Nothing, and I mean nothing, threatens a relationship more than broken trust. Trust is the heart and soul of a healthy relationship, the very glue that holds it together. But a fire relationship can certainly veer into unhealthy behaviors. So what happens when your trust is broken? What if there is infidelity? Financial lies or drug use?

My God, I've heard some pretty devastating stories in fire marriages, and I'm here to tell you that I've also experienced some real valleys in my own as well.

The fact is, many of us have had our trust broken to varying degrees in our relationships—maybe you spent too much on the Visa and tried to hide it, or maybe they lied about an addiction, or, worse, someone was unfaithful. Nothing is more painful than when you've been betrayed by your other half.

However, only you can decide whether your relationship is repairable, and only you and your partner can decide the next steps to take. Many relationships fall by the wayside at such times, and yet many couples have climbed back from what might have seemed like a lost cause.

Where there is remorse and a willingness to stay together, there is hope. Even so, rebuilding trust may take years. After all, your relationship has been shaken to its foundations; like an earthquake, such damage will take a long time to rebuild.

Here's what you need to know about rebuilding trust:

First of All, It is Possible. Relationships sometimes go through some pretty heavy stuff, all of which is soul-wrenching. If there is a sincere desire to work on the relationship, then it is possible to rebuild trust. First, seek out a counselor, clergy member, or other professional to begin the process.

Put Truth on the Table. There is no way trust can even begin to be rebuilt unless everything, as a first step, is put out on the table. If either you or your spouse has had their trust broken, then there needs to be a lot of patience. During this vulnerable time, asking questions and seeking reassurance is a must. That will continue for as long as it's necessary.

Open the Lines of Communication. During a time of broken trust, one person may be afraid to speak honestly with the other for a variety of reasons. By allowing one another to openly communicate your needs without judgment, you will begin the true process of intimacy.

The word "intimacy" sounds like "In-To-Me-See." It's a beautiful invitation to really look into your partner's heart and provide a safe place for that vulnerability. Think about where you may have played a part in contributing to the breakdown of your relationship.

Make time to talk, talk, talk. Make a commitment to prioritize putting each other first. Set goals and expectations.

You'll also want to set up some rock-solid boundaries. These may include not hanging around certain people who have an unhealthy influence. It may include things like allowing each other access to social media accounts and text messages. If both of you are committed to rebuilding trust, then there can be no secrets. If your relationship is to be saved and trust is to be rebuilt, then this will not be an issue.

Practice Forgiveness. Couples have to make a decision at some point to stop bringing up the past and move on. If you and your partner have decided to rebuild your trust, then you must commit to moving toward a better future and letting the hurt go.

A Psychic Separation. Sometimes in a relationship, commitment is all you have. During my marriage's winter season, I developed a coping mechanism for myself that I called a "psychic separation." I didn't actually leave our home or make my husband leave. Instead, I took a much-needed mental break from the turmoil our relationship was creating while still living together.

I told my husband that for now, my only focus would be on the happiness of our children; I just needed time away from him, both emotionally and mentally. And though this may not work for everyone, it certainly helped me. I guess it's kind of like "a marital ceasefire": mutually agreeing to step away from the conflict.

Taking a psychic separation allowed us the time to clear our heads and take a respite from our crisis. We held absolutely no expectations about what our next step was going to be. It allowed us to simmer down, and, since we didn't do much conversing, have that time and space to imagine what life would be like without each other.

For us, the time between when I took that psychic separation until we grew back together was a couple of months.

The Big Choices Stage

This is the fork in the road of your relationship. You both know that you cannot continue your relationship the way it's going; you are either going to make it work or you are not. This is the stage where you begin to weigh the pros and cons of staying married or getting a divorce.

For me, I knew deep down that I loved my husband and that the two of us had let "stuff" cloud the goals of our marriage. We had neglected our marriage, and we decided to start getting back on track through counseling. I've actually been down this road many times!

It's worthwhile to remember what you once loved about your partner and the early dreams the two of you shared to give you a glimmer of hope. You may feel both confused and uncertain as to where you can start, but just making the choice to work things out is a step in the right direction.

If a couple does decide to separate, either temporarily or permanently, it is important that the children are not put in the middle or asked to take sides. You may have your reasons for not liking your partner, but if you teach your child to hate them, they will learn to hate a part of themselves.

The Bridge Stage

This is the stage where each person has agreed to try and make things work. The bridge represents the two of you meeting in the middle. This is a fledgling stage. It's about moving towards your partner so the two of you can reconnect.

For my husband and me, it came after our psychic separation.

If you have decided to go to counseling, you're probably feeling overwhelmed with all the new information you've received. Maybe you've never learned how to communicate your feelings or speak your truth assertively. Maybe you've been bottling up your resentment and now need to take baby steps towards releasing it. It's going to take time.

Before you can get to the next step, however, self-reflection is going to be necessary. You can no longer just blame your partner for everything that has transpired. It's empowering to self-reflect with the goal of becoming better. If there is no self-reflection, you cannot make a meaningful change, and there won't be a lasting reconciliation.

The New Skills Stage

This is the stage where you apply the knowledge derived from some form of outside influence, whether it be from classes, books, or a counselor.

For Tom and me, sitting down with a counselor was a relief, because we were able to talk about what we were going through with an unbiased third party.

Once you talk it out or "empty your cup" (a saying that refers to getting all that is upsetting you out before putting new stuff back in), you can then begin the process of practising all that you've learned. The two of you can work together on a common vision for what you would like to see happen in your marriage. Let the mending and the real work begin.

How to Perform Relationship Surgery: While a psychic separation is about taking an emotional break from your partner and making no immediate future plans, performing relationship surgery is when you and your partner have made a decision to do the work necessary to stay together. To solve your issues, however, you can't just skim the surface of your problems. To begin the process, you've got to go deep.

To start, decide what the issue is and when it started.

Get to the reasons *why* it started and ask yourself whether this pattern keeps repeating itself. Did you both get too busy, lazy, or complacent in your relationship? Or maybe a crisis exhausted the two of you, and you lost your marital way.

What personality trait is preventing you from progressing in this part of your partnership?

Upon self-reflection, what area in your life would you like to change? Then determine how you can go about making these changes. Might individual counseling help?

Pinpoint what it is that you would like to see in your relationship, and then think of ways you can incorporate it. How can you get to where you want to be? What personal habits or issues need to be replaced to get there?

The Evolution Stage

Here is where everything you've committed to try with your spouse is beginning to show results. It feels good. You feel like your relationship is getting back on track and bearing some good fruit.

It's been a long road, but the maturity of seeing one another as human beings with their own needs is rapidly taking form. The skills you've learned and the wisdom you've garnered actually work, and your relationship is feeling possible once again. Hope is in the air.

The Juicy Peach Stage

This is what I call the "juicy peach" stage of a relationship. Anyone who has ever bitten into a ripe and juicy peach can attest to the fact that it is like a little piece of heaven in your mouth.

The interesting part about a peach tree, however, is that it takes years of cultivating before it even begins to produce those perfect peaches. Not only does it take extreme patience, but it also takes real tend, because it's a sensitive and delicate tree that involves lots of trial and error. However the future result, a tree filled with ripe juicy peaches, is worth it.

Hmm, does this sound like a relationship to you?

This is the stage where the two of you, after lots of hard work, are now in sync. You understand each other. You've learned how to let the little things go, and you are each far more accepting of the other.

This is the mature stage of a relationship (though you both might still be quite young). The two of you "get" each other, and you both no longer try to make the other change. You really appreciate that life is too short to be petty about the small things. The family you have grown and the dreams you share are now ready to take off. Believe it or not, this is when the real fairy tale begins.

We often believe that the ideal fantasy is at the beginning of a relationship. Oh, no. You have to go through the tough times, learn new skills, set clear goals, and grow as people to get to the best part ... the juicy peach stage. Aren't you glad you grew and got through?

Getting Real About Perfect Relationships

Ever since I was young, I have been fascinated by good marital relationships. I used to keep a scrapbook of famous couples I admired and I tried to figure out what it was that kept them together. Quite a sophisticated hobby for a little girl, I have to say.

The problem, however, was I actually thought marriage should be all wine and roses. Because I had no successful marriage role models, I didn't know otherwise.

Though I carried the dreams of that romantic little girl into the beginning of my marriage, when reality set in, I found myself believing what I'd learned from my family's committed relationships: that we would break up.

To get over this feeling that we would separate every time we had a disagreement, I had to educate myself about healthy marriages. I learned about love languages, the male and female brain, and birth order. I also asked couples—the ones whom I thought seemed happy—what the secret for their long-lasting relationships were and how to persevere.

Here's what I really want you to know: having a great relationship is not just for the lucky few who have found their "soul-mates" and lived happily ever after. Having a great relationship is for everyone.

The idea of having a trouble-free relationship, however, is preposterous. Some couples might fall into the trap of likening their relationship to that of other couples', or to a Hollywood movie, and therefore think that everyone has it better than they have. We wonder, "Why can't I have that? What's wrong with my relationship? What's wrong with my spouse? What's wrong with my family?"

There is no such thing as perfect relationships, families, or people. I categorically comprehended this most treasured lesson many years ago, when my husband and I were with our kids on a holiday in Whistler, British Columbia.

It was a hot day, and our family of four rented some bikes to ride to a lake near our resort. I had my youngest in one of those bike trailers behind me, and he screamed and cried the entire time because he was too hot. It had already been a challenging morning, so this episode made me feel even more like a terrible mom.

When we arrived at the lake, I spotted what looked like the perfect mother. She and her son were playing peacefully on the edge of the shore, tossing rocks into the lake and speaking sweetly to each other.

Not my family.

While my hubby and our elder son also collected rocks to skip on the lake, I sat on the beach with my cranky younger son, wishing I could simply go back to the hotel, alone.

However, as good luck would have it, after a few minutes, this perfect mother sat beside me on the beach and we struck up a conversation. As the two of us talked, she admitted something that changed my entire outlook on what I thought I knew.

"My kid is driving me nuts," she said. "It's been a long, tough day. Can't I just be alone for five damn minutes?"

Oh my God, what did I just hear? What I had conjured up in my head about her having a stress-free, perfect life wasn't even real! I was very relieved at what this honest mom had shared with me. Do yourself a favour and remember this story the next time you assume something about other people's "perfect" lives. Nobody is perfect, not even if they pretend to be.

What Do You Have to Lose? A Lot.

My pastor, and her husband had a horrible marriage in their early days, and they were on the brink of ending it. However, they decided to "turn their sinking ship around," work on it, and focus on making a better marriage.

When her husband walked their twenty-five-year-old daughter down the aisle, my pastor burst into tears at how far they'd come. Had they quit their marriage years earlier, they would have been dealing with a laundry list of unresolved resentments, possibly including requesting special seating arrangements at the wedding reception.

I think you get the picture. When we end our marriages just because we're angry or resentful, those feelings never get resolved; they just carry on.

Chris: Ex-Fire Wife

Chris, now an ex-fire wife, ran into the same challenges that many fire couples face. Unfortunately, her marriage ended in divorce.

"Our problem was a huge lack of communication—that plus we spent so much time apart doing our own thing. I got used to relying on myself and just learned to set up my own life because my husband wasn't always available."

However, Chris felt like she had been kicked in the gut when her husband tearfully confessed that he'd had an affair with a female colleague.

"I felt sick," Chris said, "and I wanted to throw up. We went to counseling, but I just couldn't get past the hurt that the picture of him with someone else created. The guys used to tease him and say that I was just jealous he loved his job so much, but nothing could be further from the truth. I just missed my husband, and we got caught up in a vicious cycle."

"In hindsight," she continued, "I could have done more to save our marriage before it got out of hand. But we just let it get out of control. We both regret not working it out now, at least for the kids.

"He got remarried and had another child, but I hear he and his wife are going through some tough times. The kids are doing all right, but not great. There are just so many more people we have to deal with now, and sadly the kids now feel like I used to—last on the list."

Marie: Fire Wife Married Thirty Years

Today, Marie is very happily married to her firefighter, but it wasn't always that way. Here, she remembers one particularly rough patch in her marriage.

"Before my husband and I made affirmative changes to our marriage, I used to hear the old Peggy Lee song 'Is That All There Is?' playing through my head whenever I looked at my husband. He would be sleeping—again—after he had worked all week, volunteered, and then hung out with his brothers for breakfast after a night shift.

"Actions speak louder than words and, as far as he was acting, it was the fire brotherhood first and our marriage second. His loyalty to the department was putting me, his wife, on the back burner. It really hurt. Things had to change if we were going to stay together.

"You know the old saying, 'When mama ain't happy, ain't nobody happy'? Well, I wasn't happy.

"Fortunately, knowing what I have now and how much better it can get, I'm glad I didn't give up too soon. With plenty of advice and some good counseling, I was able to make a plan to get our marriage back on track. But let me tell you, I thought of calling it quits more than a few times over the years. Now, thirty years later, we're better than ever. But you need a direction for your marriage, and that direction needs to come first.

"He didn't realize he had gotten caught up in being busy, so we began to focus on balance. It's easy for these guys to get carried away—a complaint I hear from a lot of women married to firefighters. These men love their wives—they just need to be reminded that their marriage should come first.

"We could have been another statistic, but I'm glad we're not. I get goose bumps just thinking of how close we were to breaking up.

"Today, we're best friends, and while we both still have the freedom to spend time doing what we love, I've learned to let him sleep off his shift so we can spend more time having fun together. And he's learned not to take on too much. We're both happy with that."

Standing Strong Tips from Marie

You Can't "Microwave" a Good Relationship. In this era of instant gratification and having everything at the click of a button, there is no app to fix your relationship in an hour. You can't get your money back if it doesn't work out in thirty days. To be successful in a relationship requires patience, understanding, forgiveness, love, and, most of all, a will to make things work.

Remember, You Made a Commitment to Your Partner for a Reason. That's because you loved them and wanted to spend the rest of your life with them. You quite likely stood before your family and friends to make this commitment. Step back and make the effort to be accountable. Remember why you are together and how you got there.

The Nest Will Be Empty One Day. Your partner will retire, any kids will have grown up, and the two of you will enjoy a whole new phase of your relationship. Don't give up on that gift. Enjoy your present relationship and remember there is a lot of good stuff on the way.

What I Wished I Knew Before I Got Married

I wish I had known that the very best relationships are always the ones that make it through the toughest of times. Your wedding day is the beginning of the most challenging, intimate relationship you will ever have. And despite all the ups and downs that you will go through, it will be worth it.

If you want the best relationship ever, one that is mature, romantic, caring, and committed, then you must tend to it like a garden: cutting away what no longer works to bring beauty, and then planting more of what you'd like to see.

When you're conscious that every stage needs attention, your relationship will grow into something truly extraordinary. Time and time again, we will have to go back to the beginning to remember who we were, once upon a time—only now we're even better.

96

CHAPTER FIVE

Standing in Your Shoes

Blessed be she who is both furious and magnificent.
TAYLOR RHODES

Being Strong in the Most Challenging of Relationships

First of all, can I just tell you how proud I am of you? Being a fire wife is no easy task, but the truth is, you're made for it. Compared to the average person, you possess more strength and courage than most.

However, being strong and courageous doesn't mean you feel brave and powerful all the time. So here is a question I'd like to ask you: if, at this moment, you could tell your firefighter the harder parts about being married to them, what would you say?

Perhaps you've felt second best after their brothers and sisters in the department? Would you say that you are feeling lonely and worn-out from going to school events and family functions on your own year after year? Does their occasional emotional detachment make you feel scared or, even worse, insecure? Or would you tell them that you are tired of their mood-swings and having to sacrifice your independence to keep things running well at home while they're away?

The other day, my hubby and I had a huge marital break-through. We went for what I thought would be a romantic lunch when, out of the blue, he said, "Hon, you've got to start bringing more money into the household."

For a moment I sat stunned. Not because I didn't want to bring more money into our home, but because I'd put my entire career on hold to support him becoming a firefighter—thus, there wasn't any big money in the household. Had he forgotten this?

Normally I would have just absorbed his words, inevitably leading to a feeling of worthlessness. But not this time. Something fierce rose up inside me: a confidence about the invaluable role I have played in our family, and a deep-seated awareness that our children were well-adjusted and happy in large part because of me.

Clearly and assertively, I reminded my husband of his oversight. He never brought it up again.

After lunch that day, I felt like a weight had been lifted from my shoulders. The truth will set you free, and it certainly did for me.

Your reality needs to be valued, and in order for your fire-fighter to look after their relationship and respect your wishes, they need to hear what you have to say. When they understand what you go through, they get to know you—not just you as their partner, but as a person; they get to know your heart.

When You've Put Your Dreams on Hold

As you know, I experienced this frustration when my husband pursued his dream of becoming a firefighter just as I was gaining momentum for a five-year media and communications course.

The disappointment I felt was crushing, since my dream, and five-year plan were about to be disrupted. In many ways, I felt ripped-off.

At the time this happened, we had a two-and-a-half-year-old little boy and another one on the way. Though my husband urged me to continue with my school plans, being a realist, I knew that having us both stressing over exams while trying to raise children at their most demanding ages wouldn't make for a happy home life. Other people might be able to do it, but I knew it wasn't right for us. I didn't want to throw my young family into a state of instability just so their parents could achieve their long-held dreams.

First Things First: The Law of Order

After we made our decision and my husband and I were adapting to these new changes, I received a phone call that would not only transform my thinking but also change my life. It was from my very wise eighty-year-old Aunt Jean. She put my plight into perspective.

"Tara," she said, "your dreams won't go away. You'll have lots of time to pursue all those things when your kids are a little older. Don't miss this time with them. You will never get it back, and your dreams will always be there—they'll wait for you."

Aunt Jean's light-hearted, though sensible, words put me at ease.

Now, you'd have to know my aunt to realize why I took her words to heart. First of all, she was a creative person who wrote environmental books way ahead of her time. Secondly, she was a very powerful personality who, with four adult children, had regrets of her own.

My aunt's advice really inspired me; it came at the perfect time. What if she hadn't called? Would I still be bitter and panicked? Probably. But it was meant to be and I saw it as a sign. My beautiful Aunt Jean took the urgency out of my need to accomplish something right that minute. Besides, my other dream, the one of being a mother, was right in front of me.

The lesson I learned that day was significant. It taught me not to rush through life, and instead live in gratitude for where I am planted right now. I also learned to put first things first and, as it turned out, life has flowed much smoother since.

I call putting first things first the Law of Order. When we practice the Law of Order, it means that we don't put the cart before the horse. We imagine the future, and we are realistic about what needs to happen first. We don't rush ahead to accomplish things prematurely.

If we rush ahead, many things that are important in our lives will be left unattended. Do one thing at a time in its order of importance.

I decided that if I didn't invest in raising my children first, particularly in those most important five to seven years, I might pay for it down the road. The way I saw it, my husband and I were essentially taking turns.

Practising the Law of Order, particularly in a day and age when everything moves at lightning speed, takes insurmountable self-discipline.

I think the root cause of rushing into anything is based on fear; when we let fear be our guide, nothing ever works out. When we take the time necessary to do first things first, the outcome will have lasting effects.

Going through some of my old journals, I came across this little note I wrote to myself after my conversation with my aunt:

When my children are older, I will have the opportunity to see my dreams take off full throttle. And what will be so wonderful and sweet about my success is that I will have an emotionally, spiritually, and mentally healthy family to share it with. It's not worth it to me to skip past the predestined "seasons" of my life. I will embrace them to become a full-hearted woman with no regrets.

Grow Where You're Planted

If you find yourself in the position of having to "take turns" in your fire relationship, determine what you can do now with where you are in this moment.

After my husband and I made a decision that was right for our family, I knew I could still work towards my goals a little at a time. And because I knew to put my priorities first, opportunities just seemed to find me with very little effort.

While I worked from home part-time to bring in extra money, I also took a course to be a Virtues Project facilitator. I worked a few times a month speaking to parents at parent-participation preschools. Additionally, I was invited to write an opinion column in our local paper after I sent a letter to the editor. I then created and put on a yearly women's conference in our city, where most of the planning could be done from home until the big day; all those parties I'd hosted came in handy!

As the years went on, I saw how instrumental all of this experience that I was accumulating would be to my future endeavors. I grew where I was planted and it paid off.

While you may not be able to do everything right now, get started on the things that will move you towards your dreams. Make sure they are things you know you can fit into your schedule. Can you start a blog, sign up for a community class, or take an online course to work towards a degree? Sit down with yourself and make a list of what you'd like to start, and then get going.

Feeling Overwhelmed

Even when you work full-time, you will, as a fire wife, still seem to look after the bulk of the household and family responsibilities. Fortunately, when our firefighters are home and aren't sleeping, for the most part they're great at pitching in. However, by the sheer fact that they work shift, you'll be left on your own a lot.

The irony, of course, is that when you need your partner most, the chances are pretty good that they'll be busy saving, volunteering, or helping other people. Here is when as a fire wife you will begin to feel not only worn out, but overwhelmed.

One of the things I honestly had to do to stop feeling overwhelmed was to lower my standards. There were times I just didn't have the energy to take my son to his third lacrosse practice or game of the week. Instead, we'd all stay home, watching movies and eating popcorn in bed. My husband wasn't happy about that, but, oh well—it kept me sane.

I'd also really let it all hang out on the nights my hubby was at work. He worked his extra job in between his two 14-hour night shifts. When I wouldn't see him for two nights and one day, I'd slack on my housework a little, order a pizza for the boys and me once in a while, and then get everything organized the night before Tom was due home.

Hell, you've got to do what you've got to do to stay happy.

When you start to feel overwhelmed, you've got to know when to call it a day. Too many people try to be a superhero, and it's not worth it if you're going to burn out into exhaustion.

If you're burned out, you won't be able to do anything well. Besides, the pace of today's lifestyle is not normal: it's crazy and unreasonable.

Also, this is a really good time to get to know your community. For instance, is there someone you can share carpooling duties with? And what about having one night out a week just for yourself: go to the bookstore, attend a lecture series, play soccer, or do whatever? Talk to a friend, another fire wife for instance, who's also feeling overwhelmed and see if the two of you can help each other out once in a while.

One thing I used to do was have friends over for lunch or dinner when my hubby was at work. I didn't like leaving the house and getting a babysitter all the time, so I thought, "Why not bring my community to me?" We'd have a potluck, or just make something simple like a big salad to enjoy on our back deck with a friend or two.

Sometimes the housework has to wait while you play with the kids or lie down for a nap. I've tried carrying on when I've been exhausted before, and I either end up super bitchy or in a pile of tears.

Also, please get rid of any guilt you may experience for taking care of yourself. You will feel a hundred percent better when you do. Permission is granted to lower your standards!

Worry and Fear

There are many things we fire wives fear. We may fear for our partner's personal safety while on the job, and for their mental and physical health. We may fear being on our own so often, the unpredictability of fire life, or just generally fear for our future.

We all have fears from time to time; that's normal. What is not normal is languishing in fear, because it steals the joy each day holds for us.

In 2010 when my husband was sick, I felt fear as I'd never felt it before. I feared for our future, I feared we would not have enough income, I feared my husband would never get better; I feared our life would never be good and normal again.

Fast forward ten years, and my husband is healthy, our kids are doing really well, and we went on our dream trip to Europe! All those years ago, I would never have imagined that we'd be peaceful and happy again, but we are.

When we fear a particular outcome, it's important to first decipher whether the outcome is possible or imagined. Change what can be changed, but don't be controlled by things that might never happen.

To start with, take a good honest look at what your fear is. Then, be proactive. Turn the fear around and take the necessary steps to arrange for the security you need, be that financial security for the future, education to upgrade your skills for another job, or something to safeguard your home so that you feel secure when your partner is working nights and you are on your own.

We can't control the future, but we can enjoy our lives day-to-day, have a plan for emergencies, and know that we are strong enough to deal with things as they arise. As for my husband and his profession, he has chosen a career that he absolutely loves. Yes, there are dangers, and I get concerned about his health, but you know what? He's a happy man, and seeing him doing what he loves makes me happy too.

When You Feel Like You Live Separate Lives

Being a couples-oriented person, I found that doing things without my husband to be a really tough adjustment. Whenever we were invited out with couples who weren't in the fire department, I found myself declining over and over again. My hubby was at work and I, like many others, didn't feel like joining in a couples' night on my own. When my husband did have time off, say on a Tuesday, most people were at work.

The only people who seem to understand this stuff are other fire wives. I found enormous reassurance in talking to them because they were all going through the exact same thing.

Of course, finding time to be with old friends and couples separate from the fire department is a good thing, so make sure you set aside some dates on your calendar. The fact is, it's just easier to hang out with other people who share the same shift as your partner. And while you'll want your own independence from your spouse's fire life to enjoy your own friends and interests, just be careful about living completely "separate lives."

Not integrating your social lives fosters disconnection, and it is very detrimental to a relationship. I have seen a number of couples just start doing their own thing without including each other. Before you know it, ten years have passed and they are living separate lives. Becoming that separated leaves a gap large enough for others to come between you.

It takes a conscious effort to connect often as a couple and to share in each other's worlds. If that means going for a hike together on a Tuesday or out to a movie Wednesday afternoon, then you have to make that attempt.

However, it can still be useful to check your partner's schedule and see when they get a weekend off. Check with some of your old or new friends and get a dinner party going, even if you have to plan it two months in advance.

Making sure that you and your firefighter spend quality time together to stay connected is really important. Your partner should know your friends and you should know your partner's as well.

Feeling Out of the Loop

Speaking of separate lives, once upon a time, my husband and I hosted lots of fire parties at our home; we went to lots, too. Then one horrible year, some serious stuff hit the department and put a damper on the morale. My way of emotionally dealing with this roller-coaster of department drama was to withdraw from social events. My hubby, on the other hand, carried on and went to every event and party.

Before I knew it, a couple of years had gone by and my hubby knew a whole generation of firefighters and their partners that I didn't. This was a really strange time in our marriage. When I did join my husband, he introduced me to a ton of people whom I'd never met, but they all loved my guy! I started to feel like I was the new person being introduced, and it felt so odd.

After bringing this up with my husband, it turned out my hubby was tired of going out on his own. Deep down, I knew I couldn't stay out of the loop and away from social events forever.

However, I did want us to do *other* things as a couple apart from fire functions. So my hubby and I compromised. Knowing I had to make more of an effort to join my husband at events than I had in the past, we talked about the events we both wanted to go to and the ones that we didn't.

Coming to terms with what happened at the department and our new normal was imperative. I realized how important it was for me to not only be a part of my husband's life, but also to embrace my fire life again: maybe not as I'd always known it, but as it was now.

Life is constantly changing, and that includes some of the friendships we have had. It's just a fact of life, and one we all have to get comfortable with.

Talk to your firefighter and see what relationships they're comfortable with and which they aren't. Is there any aspect of your life they're feeling out of the loop with? What about you? Any aspect you feel you need to be a part of more in your firefighter's social circles? Only by meeting each other halfway in these situations can you stay connected.

Dealing with Insecurity and Jealousy

Let's be honest here. You're in a relationship with a firefighter, and some people have quite a thing for firefighters. And even if you are not generally insecure or jealous, you may be tested from time to time when it comes to inappropriate behavior towards your partner, sometimes from people you know well.

The way I learned to handle this was to have a very open and honest conversation with my husband about my feelings regarding certain situations. I have also had to set up boundaries with some people, and others I actually cannot have around my husband.

If you're feeling uncomfortable about a person's behavior, you and your partner need to address it and how you will deal with such in the future. If it's someone you know, as it was with my experience, then you might need to re-evaluate your friendship.

Another area where jealousy has come up in some fire homes is when wives feel jealous of the time their partners have off from work, or the fun they have with their comrades at the department. Understandably, these feelings creep up because while you are home or at work, tending to the regular routines of life, your sweetie is off playing hockey, eating three-course meals at the hall, working out, or socializing in between calls.

I hear you; I get it, and it's okay to feel twinges of jealousy sometimes. But it's important to understand that it's not a healthy place to live. The jealousy is probably just you feeling left out, or thinking that your partner has too much fun when they're not at home. The fact of the matter is that these guys and gals witness a lot of gruesome stuff and, though they may love their job, they are exposed to very dangerous situations.

My dad told me a story about the time he was having beers with a few firefighters at a pub, and he went into full roasting mode: "You guys don't do anything. All you do is eat, have fun, and sleep."

A captain sitting at the table casually looked over and said, "Yup, that's all we do. It's all fun and games until we have to scrape a body off the pavement."

I am not jealous of that. Our firefighters need to have fun in order to cope with what they see; it's the antidote to tragedy.

Now let's talk about the word *jealousy*. If you break the word down, it is "lousy" (*jea-lousy*). When I break open my thesaurus, the word "lousy" returns words like *worthless, crummy, second-rate, inferior,* and *horrible.* The truth is, this is how people feel when they live with this energy-draining emotion. The opposite of jealousy, however, is contentment. Contentment and confidence.

When you feel jealousy creeping in, you need to take the

time to investigate these feelings. What is missing in your life? Let jealousy be an invitation to do something constructive. If you are feeling jealous of your partner's fun at the hall, then it's time for you to start having more fun yourself. Get a babysitter if you have to and get out of the house for an exercise class, a movie with the girls, or even something by yourself. Allow yourself to feel what's in your heart. Then follow it and fix it.

Second-Fiddle Syndrome

What can I say? It's the truth; most people in a serious relationship with a firefighter are playing second-fiddle to their partner's career and their coworkers in the department.

When a brother calls my husband to give him a hand with moving, for instance, my husband will adjust his whole world to go and help them. And while your firefighter loves you, there is definitely a unique relationship between these colleagues, which, for many different reasons, leaves you feeling like the second-fiddle. And yet, your firefighter probably doesn't even realize you're feeling neglected.

If there is one thing I have come to learn about the fire siblings' unique bond of loyalty, it is because their life literally depends on it. So please, don't take this all too personally. That doesn't mean, however, that you need to live in the background, hoping for a few crumbs every now and then in your relationship.

When my husband and I had marriage counseling, it was actually a relief to discover that this is a very common topic in fire marriages; you are certainly not alone. Setting clear boundaries will be effective in solving this problem, and of course communication is key, too.

Dealing with the Mood Flu

Being a naturally happy person, dealing with my husband's fire-fighter moods was a side effect of the job that really did me in. As a new fire wife, I was thankful to find out that moodiness wasn't just in our home, though. It was my young hairdresser who informed me, in fact, that her firefighter dad was moody too. "In our house we call him 'Cranky Franky,'" she said.

What I loved most about her telling me this was her attitude. She was just so pragmatic about the whole thing; she didn't take it personally at all.

"Oh, after some sleep he's always a lot better, and usually pretty cool," she said.

I needed to learn this, too. I remember in those early days when Tom would get home in a mood. I would be a wreck, because I took it all to heart. My young hairdresser, however, was a wonderful teacher. In addition to learning how to detach from his moods, I'd repeat a comforting mantra until my anxiety dissipated: "this does not belong to me; this does not belong to me."

What worked even better for me and my husband was something our counselor suggested. Instead of Tom coming straight home when he was feeling "cranky" after a shift, he would stop off at a coffee shop on the way, read the newspaper, and do some crosswords.

Today, even if Tom comes home a little moody, I am no longer affected by it. I just keep in mind that after a little nap, he'll be back to his fun and happy self.

I, too, remember the days of coming home from a full day at work and a long commute, just needing some time to myself. We all need the time and space to transition. Now when my hubby gets home, I give him room and avoid clobbering him with a bunch of questions as soon as he walks through the door.

There is a time for everything, and right when your partner returns home is likely not the moment. Even with little kids in tow, playtime will be that much nicer if you and your partner transition by getting a few minutes to come down in peace. Your children need to be made aware of this too. It's important and it is possible.

When my own mother worked full-time back in the 1970s, she set up boundaries with my sister and me. She let us know that she needed her own quiet time to read the paper without us kids talking to her for at least half an hour. It took time for my husband and I to figure out what works for both of us, but this strategy does and I'm sure it will for you, too.

Recurring Emotional Stress

Fire life is intense. Hence, whatever your partner experiences, whether it's a bad call, department politics, a brother in crisis, or those unexpected setbacks affiliated with the darker side of fire life, a fire wife gets hit with all of it.

Obviously, what our firefighters do and see every day cannot be compared; however, fire wives do experience trauma from an interpersonal perspective, receiving the energy, behavior, or news firefighters transmit when they get home. The problem is, if we don't discharge this energy and let it accumulate in our psyche, we may find ourselves feeling unhappy, disengaged, or untrusting.

Now, here's the thing. You are only human. So when you experience trauma, you might get stuck in that moment emotionally. You could also find yourself triggered by negative feelings if some external occurrence reminds you of that event.

For me, I found myself reliving the instance when our friend was fired from the department for acting inappropriately while using prescription drugs and alcohol. It really shook me, and I was sickened that his out-of-character mistake cost him his career, most of his friends, his pension, and his house. And though I carried on for the most part with a joyful spirit, I also carried with me a black cloud that suppressed parts of my life.

Being an empathetic person is a blessing, but it can also be a challenge; particularly, I find, if I don't ground myself with some practical discernment. The only solution for me was to get on with it and get out of that melancholic state. To do so, I had to administer some logical, no-nonsense thinking.

It was time for me to quit mourning and start living. For starters, I had to remind myself that all of this had absolutely nothing to do with my life and life choices. Secondly, my opinion about how badly I thought it was all being handled didn't matter; the power to make decisions regarding his and his family's future was completely out of my hands. How he and his family chose to deal with it was also out of my hands. Finally, wisdom told me that I had to allow for others to experience their own life lessons and grow on their own terms.

The skill of detachment does not mean that you have no empathy; it means you don't allow your feelings to overtake you. It's okay to be all right with moving on and letting it all go. You have your own life to live.

Healthy Ways to Discharge Feelings

Whatever problem you are facing and however you are feeling about it, there is always a solution. You will, though, need a clear and creative mind to solve it. Here's what I do to clear my mind when something is weighing on me.

Identify Your Feelings. When I was in therapy, in order to truly identify what feelings I'd pushed down, my therapist had me close my eyes and slow my mind down by concentrating on my breathing.

Next, she had me name the feeling. "Are you feeling insecure? Jealous? Disconnected? Lonely? If you can't name it yet, don't worry; where you feel it in your body will be the answer."

And so the next step was for me to see where I felt any tension, beginning with my head and working all the way down to my toes. It wasn't until a few years later that I realized my therapist was doing chakra work with me.

We have seven major energy centers—*chakras*—in our body. Each one holds a lot of information about our emotions and where they are being blocked.

For instance, during one session my throat felt tight. It meant that I was not communicating something I needed to say. I realized what area of my life that was in, and I knew that for me to have whole health, I needed to have an honest conversation with a person in my life.

Doing chakra work is a lot of fun and a great area of study, allowing you to get in touch with and heal your feelings. Author and speaker, Christiane Northrup, MD, discusses chakras in detail in her book, *Women's Bodies, Women's Wisdom*. She also has another enlightening book that delves into chakra healing called *The Wisdom of Menopause*.

Of course, simply searching for a chakra emotional chart on the internet will get you started. Take a class in chakra work, visit an energy healer, or get yourself a good book on this topic to see if this kind of emotional healing is for you.

Get Support From a Trusted Friend. I emphasize *trusted*, because while we may love many people, we can't trust everyone. When you're feeling vulnerable, knowing who you can rely on is a must. Good friends are good therapy, but only if they're trustworthy.

Write Your Feelings Out. Julia Cameron, creativity expert and author of *The Artist's Way*, suggests that every day we should write freehand without stopping, swear words and all, for three full pages. We can write about anything; the process is to clear our minds. She calls this practice "morning pages."

When you write first thing in the morning, particularly if you're feeling troubled, you'll clear your mind. Soon, you'll feel more positive. Without fail, I've always found that by page three, I not only feel better, but I have also solved my own problem. Get writing the Julia Cameron way!

Read a Biography on a Person You Admire. This will cause you to feel inspired. I went through a time many years ago when I insatiably read book after book about great women throughout the ages: Gloria Steinem, Colette, Maya Angelou, the Famous Five, and Rosa Parks, just to give you a very short list. I still love reading biographies of great people.

Read up on great women or men to become stronger in a trait they possess that you admire. When you study great people, you learn more about yourself, too. As I always say, to be great, study them.

Make Some Soup! I love making my grandma's chicken soup when I need some nourishment for my soul. When I make soup, just the act of chopping vegetables and the scent of sautéed onions, celery, and carrots put me in such a good mood.

What do you like to do to de-stress? Identify something that makes you feel good, and try it next time you feel negative emotions piling up. If soup is your thing too, you can find my Grandma Bootsy's chicken soup recipe in the Appendix at the back of the book.

Virtues I Developed as a Fire Wife

I asked my friend Leanne which character traits she became stronger in over the years because of her fire marriage. She definitely thought she'd become more patient, flexible, loyal, and possibly even braver.

A relationship will change you and, if you allow it, it will teach you. Here are seven traits I have developed from being a fire wife: Courage, Discernment, Flexibility, Assertiveness, Love, and Appreciation.

I Bolstered My Courage: Because our partners put their lives on the line every day, living with courage is just a state of being for a firefighter and fire wife. And the longer you're with your firefighter, the more you must practice it.

For me, my courage really grew when my husband was sick. During that time, I had to make some big decisions for our family. I also found myself sharpening my courage when I had to protect my little boys during the big Vancouver storm of 2006, and when I had to get a big black bear out of our garage.

Normally I would have preferred to have my husband deal with these things, but the odds are with his shift work, when there is fear, he won't be here. As a fire wife, you have to get comfortable with being uncomfortable—and thus courage is born!

I Enhanced Discernment and Truth: When my husband got really sick for all those months, our true friends and family emerged. While I certainly didn't expect everyone to be there for us, it was that much more precious when the angels in our life did show up to offer their comfort and support. This experience compelled me to take a look at our life and our marriage to discern how and with whom we would spend our time going forward.

When you come face-to-face with life's big emergencies, who's got the time to mess around? It's a time for truth.

I Learned the Flexibility to Embrace Change: From my favorite talk show that ended, to the best stores that close down, to our good friends who divorced, nothing stays the same. All good things, as we know them, must come to an end. Being a sentimental person, change has not always been easy for me, but there's no stopping that people move away, switch jobs, lose touch, and retire.

In the years of being married to a firefighter—with whom constant change seems to be the one thing that is certain—I've had to learn that change is simply inevitable; I can't long for the way things once were. Knowing this has allowed me to embrace the moment. I appreciate where we are right now, and I don't take anything or anyone for granted. Knowing that change is always around the corner has allowed me to know what and who matter.

I Developed Assertiveness: Fire life has made me into a very assertive woman. I've learned that time is valuable; if I'm not straightforward with my husband, I might not have an important conversation with him for days because of his shift work and extra job.

Being assertive also keeps me from becoming resentful. If I am having a problem with my hubby, rather than stewing over it, I now know to speak up. When I held things in, I would literally feel it in my chest and throat. Now I know where the old saying, "It's good to get things off your chest" comes from.

My husband likes straightforwardness too; most firefighters do. Being straight-up has improved the quality of my life immensely and saved me so much time!

I've Cultivated My Love and Appreciation: On occasion, your spouse may drive you crazy. But when push comes to shove, reality will set in, and the idea of not having them around becomes very upsetting.

Like most people, I have taken my spouse for granted, but having had a few hospital scares with my man, my commitment to loving and appreciating him is stronger than ever.

Fire Wives Deserve Recognition

When we went to my husband's first recruitment dinner, I felt so proud of him. Seeing my hubby get his badge after five years of trying to get onto the fire department made me beam with pride. Right in front of me was the proof that he'd finally achieved his dream.

As recruit after recruit received their badge and after retiree after retiree was honored with a speech, I kept waiting

117

for the part where the firefighters' significant others were recognized for the great support they give. But it never happened.

Of course, there were a few guys who sang them praises, but it would be nice if the people behind the heroes were acknowledged in a much more formal manner at these events. A fire wife's support, encouragement, and strength are undeniably influential to a firefighter, and to the well-being of the department.

If a firefighter is content at home, the hall and the community are going to benefit. After all, their partners are the ones on the *other* front line: with them up to the minute they leave for the fire hall. Fire wives deserve both respect and recognition.

Recognizing My Friend Leanne

He who has a why to live can bear almost any how.
FRIEDRICH NIETZSCHE

My friend and fellow fire wife Leanne is a great example of why we need to honor the partners of firefighters.

When she was an exhibitor at my women's conference, she had five minutes to talk to the audience. She started off by asking us a question that I'd never heard asked before: "What is your 'why'?"

Since then, I have heard this question asked by many a motivational speaker, since the question itself is a good one. Leanne told the audience that behind everything we do, we must ask this question. Her own personal 'why' was because she had a dream to send her magnificent daughter to university. Having grown up the daughter of a single mom who cared for four children, Leanne had seen how hard her mother worked to give them a decent life. She'd said, "We weren't poor, but we certainly weren't rich, either." Leanne's heartfelt speech moved everyone in the audience that night to tears with her authenticity.

Leanne is an all-heart woman who works tirelessly. She helps the homeless and the drug addicted in her own community by providing them with food and hot coffee.

In 2015, she started a program called the "Passionate Purse" whereby she collects gently used purses for homeless women throughout the year. She would then fill them with warm gloves, toques, scarves, socks, feminine-hygiene products, and bath and dental products.

The women on the street feel seen and loved by Leanne. While homelessness and drug addiction are real issues in the community, Leanne saw a need and did what she could to make a difference to these women.

She also helped to start up a hot breakfast and lunch program; it still exists today.

The reason Leanne does what she does is because she is driven to improve the lives of others. She is a natural nurturer and a mother to many, including her own beautiful daughter—a daughter who started a charity that arranges for young cancer survivors to model in a hospital fashion show. This fire family is a true inspiration.

So then, my friend, what is your 'why'? Ask yourself, "Why do I do what I do?" It will give you a clear focus and the fortitude you'll need to stand strong in your relationship, your life, and your dreams. Ask yourself why you feel the way you do:

1) Why am I eager to accomplish certain things?
2) Why do I love my partner?

3)   Why do I stay in our relationship?
4)   Why is it important to live my dreams?
5)   Why do I work hard?
6)   Why do I feel overwhelmed, worried, insecure, or jealous?"

This word, "why," is an important one; it will sort out your priorities and your principles. We live in a digital world that can easily rob you of your individual purpose and growth. Peel back the layers of your why and you will discover what and who is important to you.

"Standing Strong" Tips From Leanne

Here are some "standing strong" tips from Leanne on what a fire wife will likely go through, how they will feel, and how, in Leanne's own personal experience, she has learned to deal with it all.

"You will be emotionally affected by your spouse's career. Your firefighter will be brought out on bad calls, and they will affect your relationship. This person you are married to is someone who would risk their very existence to save a stranger. They may be a little narcissistic at times, but with that they are also kind, loyal, and part of a brotherhood like no other. Embrace this—they need this brotherhood and *you* to pull them out of some very dark days.

"Communication is key. Talk to them about how you feel, too, and get support when you need it from fellow spouses or the Employee Assistance Program. I can't stress enough how important it is to get to know the other spouses—they will become some of your best allies!

"You and your career are just as important as your firefighter and theirs. You can be supportive of your partner's firefighting and what that brings with it, but this doesn't mean that you have to give up on your own career, dreams, or friendships. Make priorities of the things that are important to you. Remember that you matter, too!

"As wives and sometimes moms, it is only natural for us to nurture the people in our lives. But your needs are important as well. Avoid feeling 'left out' by getting involved with the fire department on some level. Volunteer at a charity event, show up to the planned social events, involve your kids, and become a part of the department family.

"You get what you give! Life can be fabulous if you embrace it. Each morning when you rise, be thankful. Remember, you are not perfect; but trying to be the best at something is better than not trying at all.

"I have found that being a fire wife has been an instrumental teaching tool for me; what I used to lack in flexibility and patience, I now own! I've also learned to love more openly, judge less, and not borrow worry. Life with a firefighter can be frustrating and overwhelming, but it is also fun and exciting and hot! I wouldn't trade this chapter in my life for anything. I have made some incredible, life-long friends, and have an endless supply of great memories."

*Larry and
Simone Davidson*

*Dean and Tara Stroup and their children (from left to right),
Maddy, Tyson, granddaughter Lexi, Janel, and Krista*

Dave and Kathleen Nadalin
Doug and Leanne Dean

From Left to Right – Firefighter Doug Dean,
Daughter Carrisa Basham, Her Firefighter Husband Tyler
Basham, and Leanne Dean

Sheila Alwell and Her Family, from Left to Right-Sheila, Daniel, Sarah, Sarah's Husband Lien, and Sheila's Husband Gerry

Tara Stroup

CHAPTER SIX

Moving from Feeling Like a Five to a Ten

Love yourself first and everything else falls into line.
LUCILLE BALL

Developing Your Full Potential Leads to a Lifetime of Happiness

A young fire wife sits with her grandmother, also a fire wife, over a cup of tea. Having been married for seven years already, the young woman opens up to her grandmother about all the troubles in her marriage.

As she listens, the grandmother notices that not once does her granddaughter take responsibility for any of her troubles. And although she could hardly think all the blame lies with her good-natured girl, the grandmother has been there herself many times in her own fifty-year marriage. She prepares to give some forthright advice.

"So, what am I supposed to do?" asks the granddaughter.

Her grandmother takes her hand and says, "Honey, you know how much I love you. I think you are a beautiful young woman, inside and out. But here's what I see. You both want a ten-out-of-ten marriage but, at best, you're behaving like a couple of fives."

It's not until we enter an intimate relationship that we discover our flaws and determine where we need to grow. Intimacy is about growth, and people bring all kinds of peculiar habits, and sometimes self-serving beliefs, when they get together. Relationships, however, are about transforming into our better selves, and we get that way when we practice self-awareness and accountability.

As you well know, at the beginning of this journey I was not too happy about being a fire wife. Having my life plans completely rearranged was very distressing and I didn't have a shred of enthusiasm for this new life we were getting into.

In the end, though, I knew that I couldn't stay feeling this way and recognized that I had to perk up and find my place in all of this. Taking steps to feel better about our new future was vital for me. For one, I deeply believe that negative emotions can make us sick. And two, I couldn't waste an entire lifetime not turning this situation into something good. This was our new reality, and we were going to have to sink or swim.

For any relationship to be healthy, especially a marital one, we have to begin with having a healthy relationship with ourselves. While it's true that we cannot change other people, when we strive to feel optimal on the inside—when we self-reflect and have the self-awareness to take 100% accountability for who we are, our choices, and our mistakes—we will not only feel liberated and self-assured, we are also better able to see our relationships with others in much more considerate ways.

Why We Sometimes Don't Act Our Best

When we don't act or feel ideal, there is usually a reason. I know for me that my health or a shocking incident can really throw me off balance. In addition, certain unresolved issues on my end resulted in me putting other people's needs over my own. Here are some more reasons why we sometimes don't feel or act our best.

- We are holding our emotions in;
- we are agreeing with everyone when we don't agree;
- we are not standing up for our beliefs, or feel ashamed when we do;
- we feel a lack of something: money, positive relationships, or trust;
- we are stuck in the past;
- we have health problems;
- we have pushed ourselves too far and are suffering from burnout;
- we do not have or have lost our purpose;
- our self-esteem has been injured by the toxic people in our life.

What's Blocking You from Your Blossom? The Road to Authenticity

And the day came when the risk to remain tight in a bud was more painful than the risk it took to blossom.

ANAIS NIN

For me, this quote by French author Anais Nin means that it is more painful to not be yourself than it is to be your authentic self. I was a people pleaser, and at one time very shy. I'd been this way since childhood, when I was trying to make my arguing parents get along and interacting with an extended family who were always taking sides with each other.

For others, personal blocks might include incorrect thinking, old unfounded beliefs, low self-esteem, negativity, and, more seriously, any kind of abuse. However, it's your right to fully grow into your true self.

In order to do that, you have to see what mistakes you are repeating over and over; you must discern the pattern that is holding you back. Overcoming these self-defeating patterns is what growth is all about. Once you discover what exactly has been blocking you from blossoming, you will have a fresh start to redefine who you'd like to be, what you'd like to achieve, and where you'd like to go from here.

If you have trouble revealing what is blocking you, as I did, again let me highly recommend finding a reputable professional to help. I went to a therapist who specialized in family scapegoating and dealing with narcissistic personalities; they helped me to isolate just what it was that was troubling me.

Although I thought I was doing well in my life, there was something within me I just couldn't reach—but I knew it was there. I remember writing to try and get to the heart of it, and even meditating to identify it, but to no avail. It worried me, because I'd always felt so in touch with myself. It troubled me that with all the self-improvement reading I did and all the Oprah shows I had logged, I just couldn't open up this Pandora's Box.

After committing to counseling once a week for several months, I finally broke through. Being a people-pleaser meant that I always put myself second. Everyone else came first. I was continually in service to other people's happiness and rolling out the red carpet for them. Trust me: there is a happy medium to have here. But people-pleasers get taken advantage of and start to feel drained because, yes, they attract a lot of people who need constant support.

But guess what? In addition to being self-aware about what was holding me back, I was able to hold myself accountable to it and take charge of my weakness to make myself strong. I grew my own self-respect.

So then, how do you know if you are blocked? Blocks often show up as addictions or unhealthy personality traits. It could manifest as escapism, such as watching too much television, drinking too much alcohol, taking drugs, or constantly shopping for things you don't need. It could also show up as anger issues (including passive-aggressiveness), jealousy, bouts of depression, or even just that niggling feeling that says you are living your life half-full. To be honest, I believe most issues stem from people not being their authentic selves.

Self-Reflect to Become Self Aware

Every moment of one's existence, one is growing into more or retreating into less.
NORMAN MAILER

In order to seize my full potential and remove the blocks that were holding me back, I needed to examine the parts of my life I'd been neglecting. I needed to understand what had been broken inside of me so I could repair it.

The past several years had challenged me with one unexpected event after another. I could see that not only had that taken a toll on me physically, it had worn me down emotionally as well. Where once I was self-assured and had healthy feelings of self-worth, I started to really be affected by external opinions, such as the shaming I received from a few cynics who didn't like the exposés I wrote as a newspaper columnist.

129

People pleasing, it would appear, still lingered deep within, and I hadn't yet grown the tough skin needed to stand against those who are egotistic.

While people did tell me I was an inspiration and a light that gave them hope, during this brief passage of my life my injured self-esteem thought, "Are you sure it's me you're talking to? Do you know the real me? The person who, yes, is full of light and joy, but who also weaponizes her words if you are brutal, a bully, or a liar?"

It was not right to beat myself up for being a woman of justice. It was time to love all the parts of me. Not just the sweet and earthy parts, but also the hard-hitting, outspoken ones too. I mean, how would I get anywhere in life if I didn't have my fierce, candid self? The part of me that calls out hypocrites and bullshit? It was this part of me that gave me the debating skills and energy to write a monthly column that was principled, popular, and (mostly) well-received.

It was time to overhaul the lies that I'd allowed to take root in my head and my heart. The irony, of course, is that I was ashamed to admit I felt shame. Regrettably, I bought into it.

Fortunately, in talking to a professional, I figured it out. Shame is an awfully heavy coat to wear. For many years I suffered in silence, allowing my inner light to dim so that I could fit in and not offend.

Just a few months prior to my revelation, my dad passed away. The hardest part in his leaving Earth was that he departed with so much regret. Though he had lived a good life and was an optimist to the end, his remorse gave me pause—and made me think about how I would live my life going forward.

I wondered, what would my ninety-nine-year-old wise-woman self say to me?

She'd tell me, "You have a lot of good work to do. Stop getting distracted. Love people, but live to delight God with your talents and deep sense of justice for the defenceless. After all, he made every part of you. When God made you with his very own hands, who could be against you? Actually, who the hell cares who is against you? You have a purpose to fulfill. Be a God-pleaser, not a people-pleaser."

That's what she would say. That's what I had to remember.

Take some time to self-reflect. What inner blocks are preventing you from reaching your authentic self? If it helps, think about your wise, ninety-nine-year-old self and what they would say to you. How would you live without regret?

Heal Yourself to Heal Your Marriage

You've always had the power, my dear,
you just had to learn it for yourself.
GLINDA THE GOOD WITCH FROM
THE WONDERFUL WIZARD OF OZ

When I stopped participating in events with my husband because of others' opinions, it began to interfere with our marriage. However, in order to regain my confidence, I needed to do the work.

Prior to making healthy changes in my life, I hadn't realized just how much blame I was placing on others. I was giving them way too much credit! And though it feels appropriate to blame others for what they've done or why we feel the way we do, we need to remember that we are the ones actually in control over our own lives. Otherwise, nothing will ever change.

To rescue both myself and my marriage, it was evident that I had to heal this part of myself. No one deserves the lingering of unhealthy emotions, especially when they begin to adversely affect our lives.

It felt powerful to be one hundred percent accountable for myself. I thought others held the key to my future. But when I became responsible for every aspect of how I felt, it was as though the power I'd given to them returned to me.

Assembling Your Team

To get started on the journey to my improved self, I knew I had to bring in the professionals. I didn't do this all at once, but rather over a period of a couple of years. After I did this, I was on my way.

Taking the first step is always difficult, because we tend to make up excuses: we don't have enough time, we are too busy, or we'll get to it down the road. But we can't have excuses when it comes to the health of our mind and spirit. You deserve to live optimally and be your best self. You won't regret it.

Family Doctor

For many years, I had a family doctor whom I absolutely loved. He was, in my books, one of the best doctors around. However, when I tried to get my thyroid balanced, it came to my attention that standardized thyroid testing in the medical profession only tests one of the two thyroid functions. The thyroid gland is responsible for our metabolism and heart rate, so for a person to feel healthy, the thyroid gland needs to be working properly.

For many years I struggled with hypothyroidism, and it took a long time to get it balanced—my thyroid was sluggish, resulting in side effects that included weight gain, exhaustion, hair loss, and cold intolerance. I learned there is a lot that goes into understanding the thyroid. Balanced hormones are important to your overall sense of well-being and living the good life.

Naturopath

By the Grace of God, I have a naturopath who values my intuition and has been instrumental in turning my life around. He tested both my thyroid functions and put me on a natural thyroid regimen. I started to see real results, particularly with my energy level. He also tested my cortisol (stress hormone) levels, and got me onto iron supplements because my iron levels were severely low from heavy menstrual periods.

I found out that I had a huge fibroid in my uterus, and I eventually opted to have a hysterectomy. While I still see my regular family doctor, I have to say that never once did he test me for my iron levels. And yet your iron levels need to be steady for optimal thyroid function. Additionally, really low iron levels (anemia) can be dangerous.

My naturopath did not charge an arm and a leg, and should you consider getting one (I recommend it), neither should yours. If you feel funny about the costs, please do more research and find one who is not only recommended and accredited, but who is also reasonably priced.

Nutritionist

I needed to add a nutritionist who specialized in women's hormones to my team. My nutritionist took both blood and saliva tests—fifty in all! It turned out that my testosterone was too high and my estrogen too low. When this happens, a person will not lose weight.

133

Sometimes, our doctors don't make these connections, and give us a one-size-fits-all remedy. My nutritionist put me on four supplements to even out my hormones, and I am feeling the improvement.

Consider seeing a nutritionist who is educated in how food and supplements can heal you naturally. Or, to save money, study nutrition on your own. I've included books and links I've found valuable in the Appendix at the back of the book.

DNA Testing for Diet and Fitness

This test changed my life! For years I'd gone back and forth between one diet and the next, and the indecision really played with my head. Finally, based on my ancestry, I found out what foods I can metabolize well.

This DNA testing revealed to me what I knew deep down all along: that I would lose weight on a high protein, low carbohydrate, low calorie diet. I always loved eating this way, but because it felt so right, I always believed it must be wrong. I would listen to others tell me how they lost weight in different ways, all of which made me seriously blue.

I also learned that I metabolize alcohol and dairy products completely. Now imagine that; I say bring on the wine and cheese!

Therapist or Life Coach

As I've mentioned repeatedly, having a therapist or a life coach can assist you in unearthing blocks that hold you back. While my husband and I have done marriage counseling a couple of times, I found that "just for me" counseling put me on the road to becoming my true authentic self.

It's amazing how many innate solutions came about given a whole hour to dig deep and explore my feelings.

Find a Fitness Program You Like

I am not a fitness expert, but I will say one thing that I know for certain—if you don't enjoy the exercise you have chosen, you won't stick to it.

I personally enjoy a variety of exercise so that I can choose one to go along with my current mood. I have a treadmill in my house I like to use when it's cold or when I'm feeling antisocial. In spring and summer, I like to join a twice-a-week group boot camp for curvy ladies, or I swim in my pool. In the fall, I enjoy my boot camp some more and walk around an urban lake in our area.

Some people love to hike, dance, play tennis, golf, or row a boat. Experiment a little to find what you enjoy, and then fit it into your schedule. If fitness isn't really your thing, just start off small by going for a walk around the block.

The best part about exercising is how it releases the endorphins that make us feel really good and energetic.

Spiritual Group

Whether you do yoga, meditate, attend a place of worship, or believe in a higher power, how you look after your spirit will support every other area of your life. In fact, I think that caring for your spirit should come first—it does for me.

I begin looking after my spirit first thing every morning. I like reading scriptures to keep me grounded and law of attraction books—together with my favorite quotes and poetry—to

135

keep me inspired. When I look after my spirit, I feel centered and positive. I'm also a nicer person to the world!

Additionally, because I find writing to be a spiritual practice, I enjoy the connection I get with other women in a writing or artist group. Find your spiritual group (walking, kayaking, worship, hiking, volunteering) and then make time for it.

Understand the Importance of Vitamins

Vitamin B12 is a miracle supplement that will shore up your energy levels. Omega 3s are good for your heart and brain. Vitamin C is essential for your body to heal and repair. Too many people get to their old age never having made vitamin health a part of their everyday lifestyle, and they suffer for it in a variety of ways.

Once again, a nutritional DNA test can show you what you absorb well, what you don't, or what your body is lacking. Your doctor can also send you in for vitamin and mineral tests.

Vitamins are imperative. Before taking or mixing any vitamins, however, contact your naturopath or doctor to make sure that they don't interact negatively with any medications you may currently be on.

Body Confidence

There's a funny line in the movie *Identity Thief* with actress Melissa McCarthy. Posing as a fire wife, she explains her weight gain as being a result of her firefighter husband's stressful job. Now, maybe there was more to that line in the movie, but when I heard it, I killed myself laughing. I, too, had put on weight a few years after my husband became a firefighter and I chalked it up to feeling lonely, worried, and stressed.

When I finally realized that it was time to take my health into my own hands, I came up with a five-point plan to stay on track and feeling good about myself. While my personal five-point plan focuses on "weight issues," please replace mine by filling in whatever your goals might be.

First—Worthiness. You are a beautiful, gorgeous human being who has so much to give. You deserve to feel happy every day, and that happiness comes from instinctively knowing that you are worth the effort. Whatever you've been through, please remember that it's in the past. Take the lessons learned, but remember it's time to focus on how to positively affect your future.

Second—Compassion. Don't beat yourself up for the challenges you face. Every time I felt discouraged about my weight gain, I had to remind myself that my thyroid had not been working for several years, that I'd had a hysterectomy, and that my iron was severely low. And yet despite all that I was now on the road to getting healthy again.

Cut yourself a break and give yourself a pat on the back!

Third—Boundaries. Cancel obligation-invitations and prioritize your goals. If you have plans that you know will tempt you into sabotaging your efforts (as an example for me, a lunch out with the girls would entice me to break my diet), then get out of them. You have to devote time to seriously getting yourself back on track.

Remember that you are undergoing this transformative effort to, sometimes literally, save your life. There will always be another party; there will always be another night out with the girls; there will always be other birthdays, retirements, and new recruit dinners. There is no end to the number of parties you could go to, especially with the fire department.

Until you feel more stable in your goals (for me, this was when I started to see a little encouraging weight loss), going out of your comfort zone might be best left for another time. Explain this to your partner so that they understand why you are doing so and that you need them to support you in achieving your goals.

Fourth—Hydrate. Drink lots of water! Some new studies may show that we don't need that much water in a day, but I have read that we do, and I'm sticking to it. When I drink at least eight glasses of water a day, I'm flushing out toxins and fat.

Rocco DiSpirito, an American professional chef, restaurateur, and diet book writer, tells us to take our weight in pounds, divide it in half, and that is the number of ounces of water we need to drink every day. To spruce up your water, try adding a slice of lemon, lime, cucumber, orange, or a strawberry. I also like to drink a zero-calorie vitamin water once in a while, too.

Drinking enough water keeps you full, your skin healthy, and your energy levels up. If you are "dying of thirst," you know that your body is dehydrated. You can also hydrate by eating foods with a high-water content, such as lettuce, watermelon, cucumber, tomatoes, strawberries, and peppers, just to name a few. Try incorporating a big salad into one of your meals during the day to help with this.

Fifth—Patience. I've learned that it takes time to break old habits and practice new ones. Give yourself credit for any small changes that you make. If you start going to the gym or walking once a week, give yourself kudos. If you start writing your book a few pages every week, give yourself a "well done." If you've practiced setting boundaries, saying no to something, or being assertive this week, celebrate yourself.

Too often in today's society we are "all or nothing" about our goals—but that is why patience for real change is so important. Whatever your goal may be, set your intention first. Only then can you begin the process of replacing what you want to change with something better.

Changing our lives takes time. Please be patient with yourself.

Giving Yourself a Big D.O.S.E. of Love

If you'd like a quick way to feel better, follow the D.O.S.E. of love diet. D.O.S.E. stands for dopamine, oxytocin, serotonin, and endorphins. When any one of these hormones gets stimulated, you will feel absolutely amazing.

Dopamine: This is the chemical in your body that is released when you accomplish something; it makes you feel rewarded. For instance, the other day I set my intentions early in the morning and accomplished everything on my list: I went out to exercise, enjoyed the infrared sauna, de-cluttered a closet, finished writing a chapter of my book, and made some brioche dough to freeze for Christmas. The more I accomplished, the higher I felt. Set your intention, accomplish your goals, and feel fabulous!

Oxytocin: This chemical in our bodies is released when women have orgasms or babies. Men produce oxytocin too, but its effects are somewhat different, and it's produced in smaller amounts.

Among both genders, oxytocin is commonly considered the "bonding" hormone, and it increases when we receive affection, come together with friends and family, share stimulating conversation, or travel as examples. Whatever you love to do with others, make sure you do it often to increase your oxytocin levels.

Serotonin: This chemical is released in your body when you live in gratitude by counting your blessings, or by doing something relaxing such as having a warm bath. Some foods, such as turkey or pasta, also increase serotonin levels, contributing to a feeling of calm or sleepiness.

Endorphins: Exercise, increasing your heart rate, good sex, and a good laugh will give you what they call a "runner's high." When endorphins are released in the brain, a person experiences less stress, less pain, and more optimism. Endorphins are considered "nature's drug," so it doesn't surprise me that some people who've experienced addiction become addicted to exercise as an alternative when they get "clean."

Creating a Timeline of Life Events

One way to appreciate what you've gone through in your life is to create a timeline listing what you've experienced. When you create a timeline of the past, you'll get a better understanding of what you've been through, what you've accomplished, and why you feel the way you do.

When I created my timeline, I was able to see which events spurred my health problems. I also came to understand what a courageous woman I am. I was proud to see not just what I've accomplished but also all the times I rose to the occasion to stand for justice and truth.

In addition to looking at the past, add as many years (or even decades) to the future of your timeline as you desire. You want to be able to see your life objectively going backwards, but even more importantly, looking forwards you can decide where you need to make life changes.

Timeline Reflection Questions

After completing your timeline and carefully examining it, what are some of the first thoughts that come to mind? Ask yourself some of the following questions about both major and minor life events:

1) When did you observe times of happiness or having felt full of life? Try to identify what it was during those times that made you feel so good. For example, were you in a career you loved, or were you feeling super healthy and fit? Pick the year and remember what you were doing then.

2) What events in life changed you, for better or for worse?

3) Where in your timeline did an event or situation change the trajectory of life for you? How did you deal with that event?

4) Who are the kind, candid, truth-tellers in your life?

5) Do you have any negative situations or people in your life that are affecting you?

6) Can you link success or failure to being around any of these people?

7) Has there been a turning point when you knew things had to change? Have you taken any steps to make these changes?

8) If you took steps to change, how did it make you feel? More confident? More positive? Lonely? Afraid?

9) Where are you now on this timeline?

10) Would going over this timeline with a good friend or family member give you further clarity or support?

Still feeling stuck? Let's take a look at why that may be.

The Practice of "Amour-Propre"

Amour-propre is French for "self-respect" or "self-worth." Having a sense of self-respect is integral to your personal development.

I have always been confident in my abilities. Achievement has never really been a problem for me. However, allowing the wrong people access to my life was something I realized had become a problem. Why? Because I always see the good in people. And, because I have a love for people as well as sympathy for their pain, I used to lack discernment.

When I hit middle age—a coming of age for most—I had to let a couple of people go in my life. I remember my inner voice whispering to me, "You need self-respect." This surprised me, because I thought I'd always been pretty self-assured. But when I really stopped to think about the issue in question, it was abundantly clear that I had allowed a number of boundaries to slip. I was the one who had allowed this behavior, and it had obviously taught others how to treat me.

You see, turning a blind eye to bad behavior was common practice in my family. Without realizing it, I had brought this dysfunctional tradition into my life, too.

When I became aware of it, though, I made it my mission to practice self-respect. I started to check in with my gut instinct about how I felt after being around certain people. Was I depleted or energized? Did I feel anxious or peaceful? Was I questioning my own worth, or did I feel better from having spent time with them?

I think in life, even though a person might have confidence, they can also be completely unaware that they are disrespecting themselves by putting up with unacceptable behavior. But just because you are used to something (say, because you are brought up with it), does not mean it is acceptable by any means. We have to question this treatment, and then address it with both truth and kindness (remember our assertive training?).

To Live the Life You Deserve, You'll Need Pruning Shears

After I studied my timeline, it became clear to me what things were going well and what things needed some serious pruning: habits, job, relationships, and lifestyle choices that held me back from a better life. Just like pruning a rose bush of dead leaves and withered roses, pruning is absolutely necessary for new, positive aspects of your life to bloom.

As I reflected on one of my unhealthy relationships, I realized that I could not truly have a trusting friendship with this person. Of course, you can't completely cut some relatives out of your life, but you can absolutely control how much you see them. This is called "going low contact."

Giving myself permission to let an old relationship go took me years to do. It still wasn't easy because we had significant history. Letting someone go is never painless, but if their behavior hurts you repeatedly, then you've got to make the tough decisions.

Prior to severing our attachment, I took note of the reasons why it had to end and reflected on the values important to me in relationships.

You can decide whether or not to move on or to go "low contact." Here's the list I made to make my decision:

A Lack of Growth. If the relationship has not grown, changed for the better, or had at least one good, honest conversation, then it's time to move on. Additionally, you may have some "friends" in your life who don't support your personal growth in any way, preferring you to stay as you were. Once again, it is up to you to decide how much contact (if any) you will have with them moving forward.

A Pattern of Behavior. If there is an unacceptable pattern of conduct in a friendship that prevents you from trusting that person (be it because of gossip, betrayal, or other hurtful behavior), it's time to let them go. However, if you are able to have an honest and respectful conversation, and there is genuine remorse, you can both decide to forgive and start afresh.

Trust and honesty are the most important virtues in a relationship; if they are not present, there is no relationship.

No Accountability. In all relationships, there are times when we each need to take ownership of our mistakes and apologize. Yet, as we all know, there are people who never do.

Since we are only human, everyone will act imperfectly at times. I love people who are real and responsible; most of us do. For all relationships to thrive, each person needs to feel respected, and in this accountability is an essential trait.

If your unaccountable person is one you can't avoid, keep a mental restraining order in mind when you have to see them; be polite, but do yourself a favor and stay away from them.

No Give, Just Take. If you're doing all the giving and they are doing all the taking—whether it be dinner invites, conversations, or counseling—and you are feeling depleted as a result, just stop and see what happens.

I'll never forget the trip of a lifetime my husband and I took to Europe. And yet there was a person in my life who didn't ask me a single question about it! Our relationship revolved around me listening to their problems, cooking for them, or cheering them on. When you don't expect much, you won't get much—that is for certain.

A relationship like this is easy to end, though, because the minute you stop providing for them, they'll easily replace you with someone who will.

Can't Let the Past Go. If a person constantly brings up the past in order to criticize and remind you of long-ago blunders, then you can start by setting up verbal boundaries with them. Let them know how it makes you feel, and if it continues, inform them you can no longer get together. If they continue this behavior towards you, you know what to do.

You Can't Have an Honest Conversation. Earlier in this chapter, I spoke about having people in your life you can be honest with—and who will be honest with you. It took me a long while to figure it out, but not everyone wants an honest relationship. It was not possible with one of mine, so I let it go.

Some people like living in denial, and they do fine in their own little world, surrounded by people who will nurture their victim-like behavior; but not me. A relationship cannot grow in intimacy without the safety of honesty. If we can't be honest, then it's time to say goodbye.

Bless Them. Do you know what my aunt used to say of the people who were no longer in her life (including her divorced husband)? "Just bless them."

I used to think, why? How can you bless and send love to people you didn't like?

Then I heard a beautiful Natalie Cole song, "I Wish You Love." If you get a chance, listen to these stirring lyrics about letting someone go. I appreciate this song because it says, hey, things may not have worked out between us, but I wish you all the great things in life; now, let us both move on.

No anger, no hate, and no resentment; just sending a person off in love. This person is neither your friend nor your foe.

I remember hearing an actress being interviewed on television. She was asked about the rumor that she didn't get along with her female co-star. She simply said, "She is a lovely woman, but we just don't have a rapport." No drama, no need to bash the other woman. It was just a simple statement.

If you don't share chemistry together, then you just don't. We cannot be our best selves in toxic or wishy-washy relationships. We are all equal, but we are not all beneficial to each other's growth. Shouldn't we then pour our energies into the relationships we find satisfying: the ones that nourish us and make us better? Now I understand what my aunt meant.

As a cherished friend once said, "There are friends for a reason, friends for a season, and friends for life."

I'll Have What She's Having

Have you ever wondered why some people break up with a fabulously gorgeous or handsome partner to be with someone who would no sooner make the pages of *Vogue* than fly to the moon? I'll let you in on a little secret: it's because some people have what is called the "it" factor; or, as the French call it, *Je ne sais quoi*. These people may appear to be a little overweight, plain, or unassuming, but they surprisingly have the attention of many. It is their combination of attributes, beliefs, and character that people find attractive.

Haven't we all from time to time come in contact with someone who exudes such inner beauty and charisma that we, just like in the movie *When Harry Met Sally,* turn to our server and say, "I'll have whatever she's having?"

How do these people differ from us? What do they focus their heart on? How do they do it?

The truth is, what they have is absolutely magical. But "they" are not out there: they are in you, and they just need your attention to be cultivated.

I believe author and investor Sir John Marks Templeton summed up *je ne sais quoi* best with this statement: "You are sought after if you reflect love, joy, peace, patience, kindness, goodness, faithfulness, gentleness, and self-control."

Everyone seeks to possess inner joy, and to feel great in their own skin. So how do we get there? Depending on a person's commitment to cultivating this inner magic, it may or may not take years of making mistakes, self-reflection, and growing personally to become a person with that kind of magnetic inner beauty and confidence.

The true secret of the "it" factor is all about strengthening your inner space to become the person you would like to be.

The Power of Inner Beauty

Our North American culture is obsessed with physical appearance, tormenting its citizens—women especially—on how to be sexy, how to lose weight, what to buy, what to wear ... you name it.

Our European counterparts, however, have a different idea of true beauty, which I discovered when I sunbathed on the shores of the Adriatic Sea in Croatia. There were dozens of gorgeously, unselfconscious women of every shape and size, lounging like queens. They were surrounded by their families, sipping wine and eating—yes, eating—carbohydrates, charcuterie, and fruit. Others walked about ever-so-slowly, maybe with a protruding belly, cellulite thighs, or bikini top doffed, to cool off in the clear, turquoise-green sea.

These women were some of the most beautiful I'd ever seen because they lacked the anxiousness that I so often see here in North America about physical appearance.

I'd never felt more inspired by the mystery of these women's inner beauty—they exuded a quiet, joyful confidence, which only comes from loving yourself and loving your life.

Which people have you admired for their certain *je ne sais quoi*? Make a list. What draws people to them? To get the juices flowing, here is a list of women I look up to and admire for their "it" factor. Oh, and by the way, some of them I've never seen pose in a bikini.

Michelle Obama is What Integrity Looks Like. It takes enormous courage to be a woman of integrity: to walk your talk and to stick with it despite outside influences and criticism. She is a woman of character, charm, conviction and nobility. "When they go low, we go high!"

This reminder, to exercise self-control in even the toughest times (when it's so tempting to lash out at injustice), is a code of ethics everyone should live by. The world would be a better place if we remembered to always practice taking the high road.

Goldie Hawn is What Wonder Looks Like. She is an optimist who loves life and people. She is well-known for her laughter and being a protective mother. With her foundation's signature program, MindUP, she is changing the world by teaching children mindfulness to combat stress and anxiety. Checking in with feelings, meditation, and practising being present is at the core of this program and who Goldie Hawn is.

Jane Fonda is What Authenticity Looks Like. She is what metamorphosed pain and regret looks like. She is what happens when we stop blaming others and forgive ourselves for mistakes made. Jane Fonda has taken full responsibility for her life. In doing the work, she has embraced every part of herself: both her light and her shadow. This is why Jane is so compelling and beautiful. Accepting that we are equal parts flawed and fabulous is what we are.

Alicia Keys is What Faith and Creativity Look Like. The only words that come out of Alicia's mouth are positive, and always full of love for others. She calls everyone her sister or brother and revels in the talents of others. Even her Twitter account says she is "dedicated to spreading light." She lives with the intention to cast a warm glow on others. She is what happens when you live on the lighter side of life!

Julia Child is What Idealism Looks Like. Julia did not fit the mold of what a celebrity chef looked, sounded, or acted like. And yet, not only did she introduce French cooking to North America, she became a culinary legend. She didn't let anything stop her from achieving her dreams. She is proof that all you need is passion and determination to get what you want out of life.

Oprah Winfrey is What Living Life Laws Looks Like. Oprah understands that there is a system of unchangeable laws by which to live life. These laws, when understood and practiced, will create a life that will exceed our wildest expectations. She has said that "I live by the third law of motion in physics: that for every action there is an equal and opposite reaction." In other words, what you do will come back to you.

In addition to trusting your intuition and following your life's true calling, self-examination is another key to a successful life. Oprah is proof that when you know that you are here for a reason, you will make a difference. You only need to study how she has lived her life, having come from very challenging beginnings, to know what is possible when you do the work and follow Life's Laws.

My Pastor, Helen Burns, is What Love Looks Like. She just happens to be one of the most beautiful women I know. When she walks into a room, she radiates sunlight from within. She is full of affection for everyone she comes into contact with. She really loves people.

She is also an incredibly honest woman, and ministers to other women by sharing her story of a once-difficult marriage. I have never before seen a pastor preach as candidly as she does. Prior to hearing Helen, I'd only ever witnessed people preaching perfection. Helen is a breath of fresh air: she is a cheerleader of other women, and will do anything for others to succeed. Her words and wisdom have truly resonated with me.

Judi Tyabji is What Courage Looks Like. I admire Judi, as a former BC political figure and author. I also admire her for her strength and audacity. She has led a very controversial life and has continued—despite attempts to silence her—to speak out on matters close to her heart. She was the reason I found any interest in politics. Unscripted, passionate and super smart, this woman is a leader, a mother bear to three children, and full of conviction.

What These Women Share. These women I admire have an inner strength that inspires people, and a warm confidence that attracts others to them. This comes from a healthy sense of self-esteem, which can only be obtained by spending the time to practice self-examination. They are clear about who they are and what they would like to achieve.

Although they've been through hard times, like everyone else, these women have chosen to rise above and make the decisions that keep them on track with their life's purpose. They don't let their past dictate their future. To them, it doesn't matter where you've come from; it matters where you're going.

Throughout it all, these people have taken the time to help and embolden others along the way. They have been known to give compliments, particularly on a person's character or good works.

Lastly, and perhaps most importantly, they have integrity. They call a spade a spade and walk their talk. Because their values match their actions, they are people who can be trusted. People see that they are genuine.

What about your list of people who have that certain "it" factor? What traits do they share that you admire? Which of those would you like to see more of in your own life?

Virtues—The Essence of a Person

Take some time to think about what virtues you already feel strong in and which you would like to practice. Try writing them down: create a table, use two different colored pens, whatever works for you to assess the differences. Here are some traits to get you thinking:

Accepting, Authenticity, Compassion, Confidence, Courage, Courtesy, Creativity, Dedication, Dependable, Enthusiasm, Forgiveness, Friendliness, Generosity, Grace, Gratitude, Humility, Humor, Idealism, Independence, Loyal, Moral, Optimism, Orderly, Self-Control, Self-Respect, Serenity, Spirituality.

How do you practice improving some of these virtues? Find opportunities to add them into more areas of your life, and then keep it up until it comes naturally. For instance, if you'd like to practice becoming more "accepting" of events, some people in your life, and yourself, read "The Serenity Prayer" every day. Make it your job to embrace life as it is and people as they are; focus on the good, the lessons, and the gifts instead.

If you would like to practice "creativity," sign up for a painting class or take yourself out to a local craft store and buy materials in your area of interest. Creativity opens up your imagination and cultivates your unique skills and talents, be it cooking, playing sports, or solving problems.

If you would like to practice "courtesy," think before you speak and become disciplined in a whole new language of words that inspire and enrich. Courtesy is behaving warmly and respectfully towards others. Everything courtesy touches turns to gold.

When you choose a virtue to work on, commit to it.

Tips to Discover Inner Beauty

Here are a few of my favorite virtues of inner beauty. I believe that when people possess these core virtues, not only do they light up a room, but they feel good within (confident and comfortable in their skin). If you want to know the true secrets to being a stand-out human being, let these virtues be your guide.

Authenticity: You can never fool your spirit. The deep-seated need to grow into your true self is powerful. In the same way that cement cannot keep a small flower from pushing through, your true self, the person you were born to be, needs to express itself. If we don't allow ourselves to grow, what we try to suppress will seep out as frustration, jealousy, sadness, or drama. Authenticity is knowing who we are and why we are here. It is being "a first-rate version of yourself, and not a second-rate version of someone else." (actress and singer Judy Garland). When we are authentic, we find our life purpose and feel good about ourselves.

Positivity: We create our lives with our thoughts and words. Thinking positively begins with assessing how we've been thinking about ourselves. Sadly, the average person doesn't speak to themselves all that positively.

Get into the habit of catching any negative words and show yourself compassion instead. When you wake up, let the first words you say to yourself be those of kindness and optimism. When positive words spill from your lips, you also leave a powerful impact on others; more excitingly, you create a life that is uplifting and self-assured. Your world will ultimately reflect all that you think, believe, and say.

Gratitude: I cannot talk about this virtue enough because joy and manifestation are the result of practicing gratitude. Your heart will be full if you get into the habit of counting your blessings each day; even if it's just because you are breathing! Gratitude is omnipotent because it gives you an appreciation for what you have right now and turns lack into abundance, both internally and externally. It's the Law of Attraction.

Courtesy: Courtesy is the empress of virtues. Utterly noble. Yet, with the overuse of cellphones and the growing tendency to ignore those around us, courtesy is becoming a rarity. People, however, crave courtesy.

When you turn off your cell phone, thank people for their service, and respect their time, you are simply practicing good manners. All human beings want to feel valued, seen, and heard; courtesy encompasses that. When you practice courtesy in today's day and age, you will be a true stand-out.

Benevolence: You just never know who you are talking to. I remember my aunt was standing in line at the pharmacy getting medications for her husband, my Uncle Ron, who was dying at home. No one else there knew the pain she felt that her husband, the man she adored, was slipping away.

Everyone in the world—though they may be happy overall or just happy-looking on the outside—has concerns that they carry. The next time you are out, keep in mind that all those annoying drivers in front of you might be rushing to a dying relative, or may be absent-minded because they are worried about a child.

Give people a reprieve and some understanding. You just never know who could really use it that day; most of the time, we all could.

Hurting People Hurt and Healed People Heal

As people, we all act less than our best from time to time. When we hurt as human beings, we hurt others. But once you make it a habit to be healthy in all facets of your life, your relationships with others—more importantly with your firefighter and with yourself—will blossom.

While this chapter isn't all you need to know about healing your life, it is at least an invitation to make healing the most important thing in your life. From your physical health to your mental, emotional, and spiritual health, you must start by unearthing any old patterns. These patterns need to be revamped as part of the process to help you live the best life possible. When we heal ourselves, we heal others. When we heal ourselves, we heal our relationships.

CHAPTER SEVEN

Looking After Your Home

A house is not a home unless it contains food and fire
for the mind as well as the body.
BENJAMIN FRANKLIN

A Home with a Happy Spirit

Have you ever walked into a person's home and you could just feel the energy, be it positive or negative?

I will never forget picking up my youngest son at his schoolmate's house after they'd worked on a history project together. As soon as I walked into the house and introduced myself to the parents, I was nearly knocked over by their bad energy. I would come to learn that the home was a very judgmental one, and it most certainly affected this young man's self-esteem. A home should be a sanctuary, a refuge from the stresses of the outside world—not a duplicate of it.

To keep those hearths burning in your fire relationship, I can't emphasize enough how important it is to make your house into a home; a place where you and your whole family can relax and rejuvenate. If your home is chaotic and stressful, it will only add to the strain that so many fire partnerships are already under. Setting a good atmosphere in your home is essential, bar none.

It does take effort, though, to keep a good atmosphere consistent in a firefighter home given what your partner brings home after a tough day.

Creating Your Ideal Home Life

Whatever your home life was like growing up, you now have the freedom to fashion your home environment any way you want. From the influences you had as a child, to the tone, traditions, and values you currently hold, your household is yours to create.

I grew up in a predominately Italian neighbourhood so I have created my ideal home life with some of my favorite Italian influences: food, wine, art, and gatherings with friends and family.

Even today, when I drive through my old neighbourhood, the Italian effect is in full swing. Older Italian men still play bocce at Confederation Park, and Italian restaurants, coffee shops, and other wonderful, diverse businesses still bustle all along East Hastings Street. I feel so at home in this neighbourhood. When I travel there for solace or for fun, I feel as though I am on solid ground; I experience *la dolce vita*, also known as "the good life!"

One of my favorite memories of growing up with all of my Italian friends was being in their kitchens. Every one of them always had a cookie jar filled with the simplest, most delicious Italian braid cookies. For years I asked for the recipe, but they couldn't really give me an answer; they never really took note of their measurements, they just made them. Years later, I did find a recipe and make them myself. You can find it listed in the Appendix.

Creating Traditions with Friends and Family

Every time the Christmas season rolled around, I, as a stay-at-home mom, would long for my working days when I'd go to our company Christmas party. Then it hit me! Why not celebrate with my two boys and have our own "company" Christmas party?

So, every year after that, my two boys and I went out to dinner to recount the year. I'd tell them, "Great job this year, boys. Here's to another great year!" Our yearly "company Christmas parties" then evolved into a night downtown and a stay in a hotel. The boys would use the swimming pool, we'd have dinner or just appetizers, and then hit the gift shop downstairs in the hotel lobby.

Another fun tradition we have at our place is a weekly dinner we call "Fat Tuesday." Every Tuesday, my extended family joins us for a feast of simple foods. When the kids arrive after school, I have champagne glasses waiting for them with sparkling apple juice and perhaps a charcuterie before we have dinner.

A few years back, my sister and I started a "Cousins Get-Together." Now we all gather a few times a year with our families for lunch, bowling, or a picnic.

One tradition I really love every November is a Christmas-wreath-making party my neighbor Sandy hosts at her home. We all gather under canopies in her backyard, which sits on the edge of a forested river, and make fresh wreaths with greenery she's collected for us. We drink hot apple cider, enjoy breakfast, and do a whole lot of creating.

Another fire couple we know, Mike and Kathy, put on their annual after-Christmas tree burning with brunch and a Caesar bar, and our friend Jeff, another firefighter, celebrates his Irish heritage on St. Patrick's Day with friends and an Irish stew. What about your traditions? Are there any traditions you hold dear or would like to start?

Organization the Firefighters' Way

If there is one thing I envy in a firefighter's training, it is their organization skills. Don't get me wrong—I like that they save people, too!

Just recently, my husband had a bunch of buddies over from the hall for a summer party. When I woke up in the morning, the house was nearly immaculate. Now, I'm not saying all firefighters are like this, but it was not the first time I've witnessed such gorgeously orchestrated housekeeping skills from this group of guys.

Like firefighters, I do have a routine during the week so that I can try to stay on top of things. And while I'm hardly like a firefighter in the housekeeping department—I mean, I do love my lazy days, especially when my hubby is away for a couple nights—the objective for me is to have a cheery home. That generally includes being organized and clean. The following tips are simply things that I do at home to make for a happy one.

Organize Your Home One Room at a Time

The ability to simplify means to eliminate the unnecessary
so that the necessary may speak.
HANS HOFMANN

I love the aftereffects of de-cluttering my home, and I bet you do, too. De-cluttering for me is also a spiritual practice, because when I'm immersed in the process of eliminating stuff, I feel very present. I also feel a wonderful sense of calm when I look at clean corners and uncluttered closets. After a while, too much stuff, too many papers, and too many old shoes piling up really get to me. When my house is mostly in order, my mind is at rest.

At the beginning of each week, I like to see what needs to get done, appointments that need to be made, and chores that need to be completed. However, I'm not always rigid about completion dates, since I've come to learn there will always be interruptions that put a project on hold for a bit.

Sometimes though, it can feel overwhelming when you think about decluttering the whole house at once. Instead, consider one room, or even one cupboard, at a time.

As a wife and possibly a mother, you probably have a pretty full schedule already—we'll talk about de-cluttering that, too! In the meantime, make a list of the things you would like to organize in each room, but don't stress yourself. The goal of focusing on one area of your home at a time is all about producing simplicity, order, and well-being.

Bring some good music into each room while you go about your tasks to make de-cluttering more pleasurable. Then begin with just one thing, such as the coat closet or the pantry. Unless you prefer to get cleaning and organizing done all at once, just do a little every day. Before you know it, you'll start to see progress.

You can also make a list of the things you don't want to get rid of, but instead repair or give new life with some fresh paint. I have always admired my Aunt Rhonda and Uncle David for revamping the same lamp over and over throughout the years. With every change-up to their home, they'd repaint the lamp!

To help you decide what to keep and what to give away, let a quote by the 1800s artist and writer William Morris lead you: "Have nothing in your houses that you do not know to be useful, or believe to be beautiful."

What can you absolutely not part with because it is useful in your home? For me, both my slow cooker and bread maker, though bulky, are useful during those weeks I run out of bread or am cooking a cheaper cut of meat.

My large home library also falls under the useful category because, although I've given countless books away, I refer to them often for information when I'm writing. To part with some of those books I loved but knew I wouldn't refer to again, I designed my own personalized rubber stamp that included the inscription, "From Me to You, love Tara McIntosh XO." I then donated my positivity and success books to high schools in my community so that young minds could be inspired, too.

As for beauty, when I look around my house, even as I sit here writing, I look for the things I appreciate in my décor: a big, artificial bouquet of colorful flowers in my living room (I love real ones too!); my photograph of a big French Mama coming out of her restaurant to satisfied customers sitting at tables outside; our family-inherited blond onyx coffee table; and my large *Breakfast at Tiffany's* wall picture, complete with faux pearls and diamonds in Audrey Hepburn's tiara.

Of course, not everyone will love my pieces, but they make me happy and reflect who I am: a romantic, history-loving home cook who adores anything old Hollywood.

Once you've made note of everything you either want to keep or donate, pick some dates on the calendar to fix your items up or drop off at a donation center. If it's not something you would ever wear, use, or display because it's too damaged, then send it to the dump.

Some of the things I found myself holding onto were, of all things, magazines! I love the pictures for my vision books, but mostly I love all the recipes. I was inspired by my Aunt Tracey, who organized hers by slipping all her favorite recipes into page protectors and putting them into gorgeous binders.

I also bought some beautiful decorative boxes to store some of my important documents and pictures. Pretty boxes make great storage units, and you can usually get them at a dollar store or IKEA for a good price.

Here is a list of questions you can ask yourself when deciding what to donate, repair, or dump as you make your way through each room.

1) What do you have that you want to sell?

2) Are you comfortable with online sales? They're a convenient way to find new owners for your old items from the comfort of your home. Decide what will go on Craigslist or other online sales forums. Remember to keep pick-up arrangements at a public and safe location.

3) Do you want to hold a garage sale? They're great if you have a number of items you'd like to sell off. If you have kids, get them to help out. Don't over-price stuff, but also make sure you're not selling some precious antiques that you'll read about in the paper the next day: "Man makes $500,000 on painting he bought at a garage sale!"

4) Do you want to take your stuff to a flea market or swap meet and rent a table? I've done this a few times, and had a lot of fun chatting to people. You make a little money, too. Bonus!

5) For the donatables, what do you want to get picked up? Here in Vancouver, I donate to Big Brothers, Habitat for Humanity, and the Diabetes Foundation. Give your charity a call and see if they offer pick-up services to save you time. Put the date for pickup on the calendar.

6) Is there a family you can start passing your or your kids' clothes down to? I have been very grateful over the years to get hand-me-downs for my kids from friends and relatives. Put the word out, maybe on social media such as Facebook, and see who's receptive to the idea.

7) What would you like to keep and repair? Be sure to set estimated completion dates for home projects, such as organizing photos, repairing furniture, painting a room, or even just replacing light bulbs. Take out the calendar and include a start and finish date.

8) What's left? If you can't sell or donate it, take it to the dump. With so many firefighters having trucks, this shouldn't be too hard to arrange!

Once you've cleared out your house (trust me, it will be an ongoing process over the years) and decided what to keep and what not to, start organizing seasonal items such as winter clothes, Christmas decorations, and camping gear with the help of large storage containers. My friend's husband used his computer to record what items they had in storage. He'd number a box and then print off a sheet to remind him of what was in each. Talk about impressive.

My hubby loves shelving, and put a whole bunch of shelves up in our garage and outdoor shed. When you put shelving up in storage areas, you can really make efficient use of a space and get lots of things put away.

Obligation Invitations—How to De-clutter Your Calendar

Now that you feel nice and de-cluttered in your home, I want you to take a serious look at your schedule. I know: if you have kids, your calendar is probably loaded with extracurricular activities and reminders for dentist appointments, school bake sales, and Parent Advisory Council meetings. Even so, please know that one of the most important things you could ever do when bringing order to your home is to bring order to your schedule.

As the partner of a busy and exhausted firefighter, don't you think that your time and energy are precious? The same goes for your time and energy as a couple. If you say "yes" to too many things that you don't love, you'll spread yourselves even thinner than you already are. Trust me: your relationship will begin to suffer because you are either not spending enough time together or having enough time to yourself.

Truth be told, when you are too busy, it's easy to get edgy and irritable, and I'm sure that's something you want to avoid as well.

So here's the thing: if you were to look at your calendar right now, how many events would you say fall under the "should do" list? My always clever sister coined a term for obligation invitations: she calls them, "obli-vites!"

Sadly, a few friends of mine live in a constant state of guilt when they don't accept every invitation. The reality is, there will always be something you and your partner will be invited to or asked to help with, like volunteer, bake, coach, drive, or hand out hotdogs. Hey, being popular is lovely, but guess who suffers when you don't pick and choose? You, your relationship, and your family—that's who.

In her book *Take Time for Your Life*, author and life coach Cheryl Richardson revolutionized this concept. She advises having an "absolute yes" list of five things you will say yes to, and an "absolute no" list for all the things you will not spend another moment on.

It takes practice to learn how to say no, especially if you're not yet assertive. However, you have to start thinking long-term, because your health depends on it. Stress can wreak havoc on the immune system, causing all kinds of ailments and disease. Human beings need downtime to relax, solve problems, set goals, and restore their depleted energy reserves.

I know some people are naturally busy, and they enjoy it. That's fine. If, however, you're noticing resistance from your children, or you're feeling worn out yourself, then it's time to re-evaluate the calendar for your own good. Pick what you love and let go of what you don't.

I recently dropped out of a club I was in because I wasn't getting anything from it. The original intention for the club was to talk about spiritual growth, but it routinely turned into an evening of women just talking about their kids. Listen, I love children, but I needed a break from being a mom to just be me and talk about my own personal development.

In the past I would have stayed in it, dreading each week and coming up with a dozen or so ailments to avoid going. But as I've gotten older, the reality that life is too short has really hit me. Frittering my time away is no longer an option. While the women in this club are super nice, my time is valuable. And so is yours. When you have free time, spend it doing what *you* love.

When you begin to free up your time, you will enjoy your life way more often. Furthermore, when you de-clutter your schedule of excess, you can then focus on those goals that you couldn't find time for previously.

Who wants to get to the end of their life having lived out a list of duties, but never having really accomplished much? It's up to you.

Cleaning Up Your Schedule

To begin the process of de-cluttering your calendar, make a list of things you want to do, a list you don't want to do, and a list of things that are non-negotiable. Please don't waffle on this. This is a new beginning for you, and one that will give you more energy and joy! Take some time to seriously reflect on these questions and write down some very honest answers.

1) What are some of the things on your calendar that you would like to no longer be part of (clubs, groups, volunteer work)? Please don't let worry or guilt be your guiding factor. Why? This is your time to be really honest.

2) Is there a friend or family member who can support you in taking back your precious time? This is not an easy process for some people who are prone to guilt or bowing to pressure from others. Utilizing a person in your life who is skilled in time management will encourage you!

3) What would you like to do with the free time you'll get when you let go of these commitments? Is there a class you've wanted to take? A home project

you've been raring to get to? Or do you need more time to relax? Think about what you've been missing out on and then begin anew.

4) What are the top five things (people, activities, etc.) you can easily say yes to? Ensure you say yes because you want to. When you are clear about what you want and how you'd like to spend your time, it's easier to say no to things that don't fall within your top five.

It may take some time to really get your list together, but once you have one it will create boundaries and further inspire you to live your values. Here's a breakdown of my top five.

God and My Spiritual Life: My faith and spiritual life are of the upmost importance to me. They give me peace and rejuvenate me. I like to sit in solitude to do my angel and virtue cards in the morning, write my feelings down in morning pages, and read inspirational books to get my head, heart, and spirit right. Whatever supports my inner peace of mind is in my top five!

My Marriage: I am very proud of the marriage my husband and I have today, having worked through our rough patches together. Today, we have prioritized each other, and spending time together is really fun.

My marriage is the most important relationship I have, so my husband and I make time to nurture it. The payoff has been very fulfilling, and we are still working on it.

My Family: "My family" includes, first and foremost, my two children. They are my heart and soul, and are the two most important people in my and Tom's lives. My niece and nephew are also very important to us, as is my mom, sister, and extended family.

It's essential to me that I create traditions and memories for my family. We share a history, and I like being a mentor to the next generation.

Creative Pursuits: From the time I was little, I've loved to write and I've loved to cook. Now I devote a good chunk of my time to doing both, with the greater dream of helping and serving other women.

My Friends: As I've gotten older, I've become less enamored by small talk, which is why my friend and I started a group called "The Gathering." Together with like-minded women, we take classes or get into great discussions on a variety of subjects.

Another wonderful group of women I enjoy being with is those I exercise with. They are good-hearted, kind, and thoughtful. Real women empowering women. I love my friends!

Starting the Day off Right

Whether it's just you and your partner or you've got a kid or two in the mix, most of us have to get up and at 'em every morning, and a disorganized start can make or break the day. When you and your partner set the tone of your day by getting organized the night before, you'll feel less stressed.

When it was just me living on my own, being organized was a piece of cake. When the population in my family grew, it definitely took more planning. Here is what a happy, smooth running day looks like for me, *if* I get organized the night or even a couple hours before "show time:"

When I know I'm going to work the next day, I set the coffee pot and I take meat out of the freezer. Then I can put it in the slow cooker before I go to work (stews are perfect for this) or get my kids to put it in the oven at some point after school. Either way, dinner is ready when I get home.

I try to make lunches for everyone the night before work, and find anything I need to take with me the next day. This keeps me from getting stressed in the morning while looking for little things like an umbrella.

I also put out and iron the clothes I plan on wearing the next day. One time I didn't do this, and woke up the next morning to find a storm had taken out our power. I couldn't see my clothes very well and unfortunately put together a very awkward outfit!

I get my kids to pack their knapsacks, PE strip, and homework the night before school. After they reached a certain age, my kids started putting their own lunches together, too.

Getting organized the night before means I can get up a little earlier and have time to myself to get centered. Whether it's writing in my journal or exercising, it makes a great start to my day.

What areas of your life can you get organized ahead of time in order to start your days off right?

Perhaps you'd benefit from having your car organized for spontaneity (prepared for all weather with an umbrella, sunscreen, and windbreaker, workout clothes for a trip to the gym when you have extra time, or maybe a blanket or chair to enjoy rush hour in the park instead of sitting in traffic).

Or perhaps your purse could be restocked for the unexpected (a snack to keep you going, pen and notepad to stay organized, or a book to entertain you in the waiting room).

Could your space at work use some more on-hand essentials, so you don't have to stop and look for things? There are so many areas to consider.

To Stay Sane, Organize Your Week

I like to take Sundays to relax and get organized for the week ahead. I take stock of the food I have in the fridge and prepare some meals in advance, including to-go salads and yoghurt-and-granola parfaits. On Sundays, I also enjoy making a large-scale meal for dinner, like a traditional roast of beef, chicken, brisket, or pork. That way come Monday, we have leftovers, and I don't have to cook!

I've always found that when I have a routine, I save money, time, and my sanity. When I'm not organized, I find myself stopping off at the grocery store several times a week to pick up costly, pre-prepared meals, and that wastes both my time and money.

If you've ever read the magazine *Martha Stewart Living,* you'll see in the introductory pages that she has her entire month planned in advanced for yard work, housework, meetings, yoga, parties, vacations, and time to be spent with friends and family. I've always found her calendar inspiring, because clearly being a super-organized person has allowed her to accomplish great things.

As I have already mentioned, I schedule time to myself throughout the day. When my kids were little, I used to take five or ten minutes in the afternoon while they watched a movie to refresh my spirit with a cup of tea, a few positive quotes from one of my books, and writing in my gratitude journal. If I felt stressed during the day, I used to spritz a bit of fragrant lavender aromatherapy over my face. It would instantly bring me to my imaginary English garden.

I've even started to get organized for special holidays a few months in advance, too. So rather than trying to organize

Christmas in a few weeks, I start earlier with deep cleaning, stocking the bar, and buying hostess gifts on sale. This allows me to go at a nice, slow pace! I want to enjoy my life and the holidays. If that means starting early so I can relax during those busy times, then that's what I have to do.

Take some time to think about what each day of the week represents for you, and then make an intentional plan. Listen to your inner clock of what days you like to do what.

For instance, Mondays for me are usually a little slower after the weekends, so I don't like to schedule things. I take that day to just come home and have leftovers with the family. As the week picks up and my energy returns, I'm better able to schedule things in.

Once you get into the routine of this, you'll really notice how good it makes you feel and how much smoother the weeks ahead will be for you and your family.

Get the Kids to Help Out

While I couldn't ask for better kids than mine—honestly, they help me with anything I ask them—I do wish I had been a more consistent parent when it came to them picking up their clothes, hanging things up, and so forth. Not only would it have helped *me* with scheduling my days, but it would have benefitted them as well: learning to be organized as a young child is an important skill to have. It teaches them about responsibility and teamwork (highly valued skills in the fire department), and hones skills like time management for doing homework.

If you have kids, getting them to contribute to keeping the family home organized means that you will need patience. Don't overreact if your young one spills the milk, breaks a plate, or drops a basket of laundry down the stairs. Learning life lessons only comes after breaking a few dishes and spilling several glasses of sticky substances. If you take the opportunity as a teachable moment and allow your kids the room to learn, you will grow very confident human beings who see mistakes as simply part of being human.

Age-Appropriate Chores

When your partner works on a firefighter's shift schedule, you'll often be the only one around to complete the daily chores. But if you have kids, there are a few that you can get them to help out with, too. I've broken them down by age-appropriateness here.

Because my boys needed constant reminding, one thing I got them into the habit of doing was to check the "responsibility chart" in their bedroom. If they forgot to see it in their bedroom, it was always duplicated on the refrigerator door, where they seemed to spend most of their time!

When Your Children are Two and Three Years of Age: Get them to help you put groceries into bags at the store, make their beds, put toys and clothes away, bring dishes to the sink, and so on.

When Your Children are Between Three and Six: Have your three- to six-year-olds set and clear the table, help with laundry, feed pets, take out recycling, and help with meals that are easy and supervised.

When Your Children are Six to Eight: This is a good age to introduce a chore chart, so they can read it themselves. Get them to help with easy meal preparation such as simple chopping, take out the garbage, and recycling.

When Your Children are Eight to Eleven: Unload and load the dishwasher, clean up the bathroom (such as rinse out the shower or the bath when they are done), wipe down counters, wash windows, and learn to use the washer and dryer.

When Your Children are Eleven and Older: Help with yard work, prepare a couple good meals for themselves (breakfast for instance), sweep, and vacuum.

One thing to keep in mind, especially as our kids get older, is to remember that they probably have more homework than ever before, and may be involved in a ton of activities. Our kids, like us, can get stressed when their plates are full. Be patient, and don't expect perfection. You are all a team, and it is important that everyone pitches in to keep the house comfortable and well-run.

Fire Wife Tips for Making Extra Money

As you may recall, when my boys were little I decided to work from home or part-time, since my husband's shift work and exhaustion didn't leave me much time to add a full-time income into our family. Until I could get my dream career going—and because I love kids—I had an afterschool daycare in my home while Tom was a rookie at the firehall. It was just one of the ways I brought extra money and tax write-offs into our home while he started in a new profession.

"Necessity," to quote Greek philosopher Plato, "is the Mother of Invention." My friend Theresa was definitely a Mother of Invention, and always came up with creative ways to make extra money while her boys were little and her husband worked as an electrician. From turning her basement into rental housing for international students to selling gorgeous baby blankets she knit herself, Theresa's patience and knack for saving and making money certainly paid off. Today, she owns a few properties and is now happily retired, living up-country with her husband.

Recently, I asked my equally-creative fire wife friends how they brought extra money into their homes when their kids were small and their firefighters were just starting out.

Bring an International Student into Your Home. Most communities have university students from overseas who need a home to stay in while they are going to school. Universities usually post on their websites the requirements for being a home-stay family, or you can call their administration.

Hosting an international student can become a really fun way to have your family meet people from other countries and play host to those who need a nice, comfortable home-away-from-home to stay. It pays well, and I know many firefighter couples who host international students regularly.

Rent Your House out for Movies. Movie companies are always on the lookout for locations and houses that they can use in their films. Your house doesn't need to be a fancy mansion to be in a movie: if it's a simple suburban house they're looking for, then you could get a call. Most companies use an online process to fill out the applications and upload pictures of your home.

One good way to find a reputable company is to call your city's permit department to see who they would recommend; they're the ones who collaborate with the location scouts when filming goes on in your city or town.

Have a Clothing Swap with Friends. Instead of giving your clothes away, why don't you and your friends meet up with all your old clothes, costume jewellery, and accessories like belts, hats, and nice shoes? Go "shopping" for something new to you.

Be a Secret Shopper. Sound intriguing? My friend thinks so. She gets to go on assignments to various restaurants and stores "undercover" where she'll get a free meal, a free lube and oil for her car, or be paid to give her opinion after visiting an establishment. You can be as busy as you like or work a more part-time, flexible schedule.

Long-term Investing

One of my favorite books for its philosophy on making money is called *Rich Dad, Poor Dad* by *Robert Kiyosaki* and Sharon Lechter. I highly recommend it. There are so many ways you can make money; investing in the stock market is one of those that can be either a fun hobby or a serious venture.

Many banks and brokerage firms offer "mock investment" portfolios, with which you can practice investing without actually investing any of your money. Such a website allows you to pretend to invest so that you can understand the process and learn about stocks and bonds. It's also fun to read up on companies and follow trends.

Once you feel you're well-versed at it, maybe take a little of your savings and look into creating a portfolio. Of course, you have to be patient, but if it is something that you enjoy doing, you can begin to build your own portfolio to start making some money.

As an alternative, have you thought about real estate? A friend of mine's Italian parents lived with four other couples from Italy in a rented house in Vancouver. They all worked hard and eventually banked enough money so that each couple could afford to put money down on a house of their own. All of these couples went on to purchase additional homes to rent out to others, which began their real estate investments. Their patience and determination to save money paid off.

While most homes are very pricey these days, getting a group of close friends together to purchase a condo with plans to sell it down the road is not a bad way to make some money for the future. If you have real estate dreams, but can't afford today's expensive market, maybe consider getting into the market with some people you trust.

Begin by doing your homework. Research up-and-coming communities that currently have more affordable real estate prices. If you want to invest in a condo with the plan of renting it out to pay your own mortgage, consider finding a company that will look after this for you.

Ways to Manage the Family Budget

Oh, my God, is this not the hardest thing? Trying to stay on top of a budget is not easy, especially when you love good food, new clothes, and nights out. Unfortunately, we all have to grow up sometime, and we can't spend money the way we did when we were young, single, and without responsibilities.

When my husband became a firefighter, I was seriously worried at the decrease in our income. I scoured the internet for ways to cut down on our expenditures and save. Here are some of the creative methods I found and used:

Shop at the Dollar Store. Why not save your hard-earned money and buy some basic pantry items like salt, spices, and dried noodles at the dollar store? I also love that you can pay less for everyday things like picture frames, measuring cups, greeting cards, wrapping paper, and seasonal decorations. I have dollar store pictures and frames up in my house, and they look great!

Plan Your Meals with Leftovers in Mind. Marinate inexpensive cuts of meat, do your own baking, shop once a week at the cheaper grocery store, and buy several items at a time when they are on sale. Buying produce in season will not only save you money, but will also mean you're purchasing it at its most delicious.

Shop Second-Hand and Save the Difference. When you buy any items second-hand, why not put away the money you would have spent if you had purchased it brand-new? You can bank it for a future trip or anything else that you'd like. On that note, you can find consignment stores in your area to buy up old books or nicer clothes you would like to get rid of.

Return It! If you don't already, return pop, wine, and beer bottles, then keep the change handy in the kitchen for transit—or, even better, for when the ice cream truck comes by.

Reward Yourself. Another thing I love to do is collect reward cards from stores that pay me points for purchases. For instance, I belong to a bank that has partnered with a movie chain, so every time I use my debit card, I get points for movies. I haven't paid for a movie in fifteen years!

I also collect points at a low-cost but good quality grocery store and save my points up for Christmas groceries. Points can add up quickly! Besides, who wouldn't want to be rewarded for shopping at a store when you already have to be there?

Go to a U-Brew. When my husband and I were first married, we had our wine made at a U-Brew all the time. You can make some decent wines at a fraction of the price that you'd pay in a liquor store. To be honest, I've had some really good wines from U-Brews. Just ask the person working there for some good selections according to the type of grape you like best.

Dine Out on a Dime. If you want to go out for a fancy meal, go to a cooking school's restaurant. Often you can get a beautiful three- or four-course meal for as little as $25. I'm serious! They usually serve wine as well, for an additional cost of course, but it still beats an expensive restaurant. Who knows? You might meet an up-and-coming chef.

Purchase an Entertainment Coupon Book. You can usually get entertainment coupon books from your kids' school, drugstore, or Costco towards the end of the year. Use the coupons inside for discounted dinners out, activities with the kids, car services, and a bunch of other things. The book will pay for itself in no time.

Don't forget to swap coupons with friends and family. For instance, I would always exchange my unused coupons with friends who didn't have little kids for the children's activities like Crash Crawley's, a fun kids' indoor play center in our town. We were all happy!

Make Your Own Cleaning Products. Back in the day when I was trying to save money, I used to make my own cleaning products. If you want to save a few bucks and be eco-friendly, put together a binder with recipes (easily found online) for making your own green cleaning products. So many ingredients in homemade cleaning products come from items you probably already have in your pantry, such as baking soda and vinegar. There is nothing new about homemade products: our grannies made them all the time.

Invest in a Good Freezer. Wow, next to my mixer, bread maker, and slow cooker, my freezer has been one of my most-useful investments. Having a good-sized freezer means that you can load it up with lots of leftovers, meats, and treats that you buy on sale.

Buy at a Discount Bakery—Or Bake Your Own. On the topic of money-saving investments, a bread maker is a solid one. Bread is cheap to make—it just takes time. But assembling the ingredients in a bread maker for your own bread or pizza dough takes two minutes. My kids love the taste of homemade bread, so I always keep a big bag of flour and a jar of yeast on hand. Of course, stocking up on discounted bread from a bakery or wholesaler is a nice way to go, too.

Stretching the Food Budget

When it comes to the big expense of groceries, finding a good quality store that is low in price is one smart way to stretch your budget. Getting into the routine of cleaning out your fridge before you go shopping is also helpful. That way you know what you already have, so you don't buy more of what you don't need.

As I write this, I can see I have a pile of browning bananas (I bet you do, too!) sitting on the counter. When I have a pile of overly-ripe bananas, I know my family and the fire hall will be getting either banana bread or banana cake. The same goes for leftover veggies, which I usually throw into a pot to make home-made soup or toss into a pan with leftover meat to make a stir fry.

The best method I have found to save money when it comes to buying groceries is to stop buying so much. I have been seriously heartsick at times, seeing how much food will go to waste in my refrigerator—leftovers that don't get eaten, bread or crackers that go stale, and all those fruits and vegetables that get ignored and have to be composted.

To give you some new ideas on how to use up those ingredients, or just give you some new and delicious options, you can find a couple of my favorite weeknight recipes in the Appendix.

Flyers and Fieldtrips

When my sister and I were little, my mom used to pack us up in her car, along with all the grocery flyers she had collected from the newspaper during the week. We'd stop at various grocery stores to get all the best deals. It was a great way to save money and spend time together.

Once we grew up, my sister and I continued to do this for a while, and it was a lot of fun. The two of us would go shopping together early on a Saturday morning and get all the best deals at one of our favorite slightly-out-of-town markets. We would then make our way home and stop off at a couple of grocery stores to pick up meat that's fresh but on sale.

What I love about partnering up with family or friends to go shopping is that it makes an excursion more fun. There's a lot to be said for real-life interactions. People need people, and if you are going grocery shopping, why not make a good time of it? Top off the chore with coffee or lunch out together. I mean, you are saving money, right?

I Learned from the Best

I grew up on the third floor of a two-bedroom apartment in North Burnaby with my little sister and our divorced mom—we called ourselves the three musketeers. Mom was a super-positive personality. She worked two jobs and raised us girls on her own. She was a homemaker, homebody, party-girl, and career woman. Her undeniably cheery and grateful attitude had a considerable impact on my sister and me, for we are known for our optimism and happy-go-lucky outlook on life.

My mother could have chosen to be just the opposite of happy, because like many divorced parents, she had lots to worry about in the way of finances, paying the rent, and raising two children on her own. But when I had a family of my own, it became apparent that a positive environment is quite possibly the most priceless gift that you can bestow on your family. While our little family wasn't rich in money, we enjoyed the good life, and it was abundant.

While we didn't have social media or cell phones back in those days, I never once heard from my mom, "Go outside and play. It's a sunny day." Looking back now, I realize how much Mom allowed me to listen to my own natural rhythm, and how I wanted to spend my free time—dreaming, dancing, writing, watching Merv Griffin on TV, and, of course, playing outside with my friends. To this day, I'm very tuned-in to what I need; a trait I owe to my easy-going mother.

Nowadays, too many people think they have to have it all in order to have a happy home. I'm here to tell you that it's mostly the simple and the soul-satisfying things that create contentment: warm feelings, good memories, traditions, and conversation. Now that is what I call good energy.

CHAPTER EIGHT

You Matter

You can only become truly accomplished at something you love.
Don't make money your goal.
Instead pursue the things you love doing and then do them so well
that people can't take their eyes off of you.

MAYA ANGELOU

Follow Your Goals and Your Dreams

While writing this book, I couldn't wait to get to this chapter because I wanted you to remember the most important thing: you aren't just a fire wife, but a person who has a life and dreams of her own.

Though my career may have taken the slow track because of my husband's profession, my family and marriage are happily intact, so I have no regrets.

Furthermore, there are many incredible women I admire—also married to firefighters—who have taken a similar path to mine. And while some of us have worked part- or full-time jobs over the years, each one is now enjoying her dream career and serving the community in ways that are both impactful and rewarding. Our persistence to pursue our own life adventures while navigating our marriages and our partners' shift work and busy calendars has certainly paid off.

Now I want to get started with you. Wherever you might be in life at the moment, without a doubt you have a heart that needs to be filled and a bucket list that needs completing.

In this chapter, we are going to continue your timeline by taking a look at what you want out of life going forward. To begin, I encourage you to take stock of your natural skills, your natural abilities and to consider the legacy you would like to leave. Additionally, to experience personal fulfillment and to satisfy that innate human desire to have both purpose and a meaningful life, it is extremely important to create a vision for every part of your life. Imagine how you'd like your life to unfold, imagine how you would like to feel, and then implement a plan. Only then will your dreams manifest.

You Are Gifted

Before you create the vision for a life you will love, it's good to know what your natural gifts are. You also have to know what you are passionate about and what tugs at your heart strings. Each one of us has a calling as unique as our fingerprint, and everyone is talented and gifted at something.

However, the only way to sharpen your gifts and talents and become brilliant at what you do is through commitment and practice. Author Malcolm Gladwell talks about commitment and practice in his book *Outliers*, and says that to master anything we must practice for at least 10,000 hours in our chosen area of interest.

In other words, no one pops out of their mother's womb a master. Full of potential, yes, gifted and talented, for sure, but not a master.

Think of the greatest people you admire. Now think about how many hours they've logged in their chosen field before you even took notice of them. People don't become excellent all of a sudden; they have had to work on their talent and refine their gifts over time.

Another thing I want you to remember is that to feel proud of your work and live your life's purpose, you don't need to be rich, famous, or award-winning. If you love to care and look after the elderly, build Habitat for Humanity houses, or participate in breakfast programs for hungry kids, you will make the most powerful impression just by making a difference in the lives of others.

When taking stock of your gifts and what you love to do, it's also essential to know what you are and are not good at. I know this might sound harsh, but in my experience, if you do this, you'll save your energy for greater things and be a whole lot more effective.

For instance, I am passionate about cooking, reading, learning, writing, nurturing, and hosting events, so I spend most of my time doing these things. I also know what I'm not good at: accounting, sewing, playing competitive sports, and so on, though I admire these gifts in others.

If I envied another person and wanted to compete with their talents, or pursued something because it would give me status or money, I would never be great at them. I might be good, but I'd never be great. More importantly, I wouldn't be satisfied.

I've seen so many people go into industries that they, quite frankly, were not gifted in but chose for egotistical reasons. It's been said that you should do what you love and then find a way to make money at it.

Celebrate Your Future—Creating a Vision

Imagination is everything.
It is the preview of life's coming attractions.
ALBERT EINSTEIN

When I was a young girl, my imagination led me to cut out pleasing photos of people, places, and things. I put them up on my bedroom wall, in photo albums, and then eventually in scrapbooks that I bought ritually every New Year's Eve. I'd clip pictures of happily married couples, my future dream home, beautiful photos of Europe, and how I wanted my family to be.

While I enjoyed putting my dreams into scrapbooks, I never seriously considered whether they would even come true. What I was doing, without realizing it, was creating a vision for my life.

The reality of what I was doing hit me one day when I noticed the pictures I had been clipping were beginning to mate-rialize. What started off as a sacred hobby, one that I enjoyed from the time I was young, was turning out to be a bigger deal than I had thought. It was astonishing! For instance, one year when my husband and I lived in a townhouse as young parents, I taped pictures of Tina Turner sitting by a pool that overlooked the most beautiful ocean view.

While I did feel a little silly at times being a grown woman who put pictures in a scrapbook, when the universe found us a house with a pool and an ocean view, I was blown away! Several years later, the popular documentary *The Secret* disclosed the Law of Attraction and became mainstream. What I had known intuitively all my life was now being shared with the world.

When you create a vision of what you'd like in your future, you're setting your intention. When people don't take the time to imagine what they'd like out of life and put it to paper, they're liable to settle for anything or anyone.

Once you have a clear picture of what you desire in all areas of life, your subconscious mind will naturally begin drawing these experiences towards you. Concurrently, you'll make choices (both consciously and intuitively) that will take you into the direction of your dreams.

Here's the deal about manifesting, though. You can't put deadlines on it. When you put your dreams together in scrapbooks or vision boards, you have to then leave them and let them go. I used to have a little laugh when people got frustrated at how "this whole law of attraction thing doesn't work," because their big vision wasn't manifesting fast enough. That is not how it works. Manifesting and setting goals are two completely different things.

Set goals, because those are dreams with deadlines; but for those out-of-this-world, big-picture dreams, the timing is never ours. Do it, believe and feel that it is yours, then set it aside. Keep looking at it, though. I always found that when I had my scrapbooks near and worked on them often, they kept me fired up. Know deep within that one day your dreams will become a reality.

Getting Started

To get started, pick a place to hold your dreams. I prefer a scrapbook because it's personal and I can close it. I don't want people making comments about my vision board if it's out in the open for all to see. My scrapbook is essentially just a large-sized, black sketchbook that lasts my whole year. Use it to add pictures, brainstorm, or write down inspiring quotes, new aspects to your dreams, and any other thoughts you have each month.

Below I've compiled some questions that you can start to ask yourself. These are just a starting point: be sure to expand from here. Take your time picturing your life and get really detailed, too! The more details you have, the more you can really feel that this is yours.

- What is the vision you have for your family?
- What is your vision for friendships?
- What do you feel called to do?
- What charities would you like to be part of?
- What is your ideal career?
- Would you like to travel? Where?
- What kind of a marriage would you like?
- Can you open up a bank account for your dreams? Start saving for a vacation, a new car, or a house?
- How much money would you like in the bank ten years from now?
- Where would you like to live?
- What creative ideas would you like to bring to light?
- Have you thought about your health and how you'd like to feel?
- What would you like to have accomplished by the time you are a certain age?
- Would you like to write a book, become a teacher? Own your own business?
- What character traits would you like to grow in?
- What would you like to learn? A new language, sewing, how to ski?

Really take your time thinking about these things and, even more powerfully, feeling that these dreams are yours. Remember that they will come to pass at their own perfect time.

Pick Your Personal Motto

In order to increase your motivation when creating your vision, you'll need some personal mottos, mantras, or poems to keep you on track. However many you refer to, glancing at encouraging words can instantly transform your mood and will guide your actions.

One year, I pasted the whole front cover of an issue of *O, the Oprah Magazine* with the title, "Live Big!" into my new scrapbook. It was about making that year the one to "live your greatest adventures and your grandest dreams." What an invitation!

Living big became my motto that year. It just so happened to be the year my husband surprised me with a trip to Europe, a major dream-come-true.

Another time my sister chose the slogan, "The Year of Me." After several hard years of trying to get pregnant, followed by giving birth to beautiful twins, her "Year of Me" was going to be time to exhale. She used it to focus her mind, body, and spirit back to health and a more serene state. Whenever she had to make a decision, she kept her motto near at hand. It helped her make choices that were in line with what she wanted for herself.

What would you like to focus on in the year ahead? What words give you inspiration? What poems have touched your soul? Keep your special phrases where you can see them as a constant reminder: in the car, in your purse, on your mirror, at your office desk, and, of course, in your scrapbook or journal.

Having No Regrets: An Exercise in Foresight

Back in Chapter Six, I told the story of my dying father expressing remorse and regret about how he lived his life. Taking his words to heart, I wondered what my ninety-nine-year-old wise-woman self would say to me about living a life with no regret, and I asked you to do the same. Let's elaborate on this and go a little deeper. Take some more time to consult with your future self and pose this most-important question to her: "*how can I live my life going forward so that when all is said and done, I will be satisfied, happy and spent?*" As you imagine yourself looking back over your life, reflect on what would have made you proud about the way you lived, and ponder all the wonderful things you were happy to have achieved.

Also think about any regrets you may have if you don't live authentically or with an open heart. Think about what you stand for and what risks you took.

Did you live your values? Were you true to yourself? Did you revel in your passions? Did you allow what pulled at your heart-strings be your guide to help the less fortunate? Did you spend time with people you loved and make lots of good memories for them? Have you fulfilled your bucket list? Used up all of your gifts and talents? What is your legacy?

Starting now, live a life your ninety-nine-year-old wise-woman self would be proud of.

In the movie *The Last Word*, actress Shirley MacLaine plays a cranky character named Harriet who finds out that she does not have long to live. However, she still wants a really nice obituary in the paper. She goes about studying "good" people's obituaries to see what she needs to do before she dies.

She comes to the conclusion that nice dead people have three things in common: they had their family's affection, they had the esteem of their colleagues, and they had touched the life of an unrelated person in a profound way. Harriet then goes about trying to make up for being cantankerous by fulfilling those three things, so that the last word about her life can be positive and meaningful.

Now then, consider your legacy. How would you like to be remembered? What would your mark on the world be? When people don't practice prudence, they make in-the-moment decisions that ignore future consequences. Without forethought, we leave our destiny to chance. Take the time to map out your life. You won't regret it.

Run Your Own Race

This is a life rule to live out your purpose: run your own race. Don't compare yourself with others, wishing you had different talents, different looks, or a different personality. Your job is simply to take the fabulousness that has been given to you, make the very best of it, and then share it with others.

Overall, try not to stray or stay in careers that fit other people but not you. Trust me: it will drain your energy and you won't be happy. Understandably, there will be many times when we need a job strictly for money: that's normal. That's called paying your dues. However, make it your mission to find out what you would like to dedicate your life to, and then use your job to finance your purpose. You are meant to have an incredible life—one that comes from knowing what part you've been chosen to play in the great orchestra of life. When you find your true-life purpose and share and serve others with it, your life will be indescribably satisfying.

Some people are just born knowing what they want to do. Others have to really dig deep to be honest about what they love. I actually believe that everyone is born knowing their calling and life purpose. However, early influences can confuse matters when well-meaning people, whatever their reason might be, have them second-guessing their instinctive longings.

One book I found really helpful when exploring my career is called *Do What You Are* by authors Paul D. Tieger and Barbara Barron-Tieger. The book is based on the study of personality typing, founded on the Meyers-Briggs theory that there are sixteen personality types. Because of the intricate research of this study, after you take your personality tests, the authors are able to pinpoint which careers would suit you.

They also wrote a book for parents called *Nurture by Nature*, which is helpful in supporting our children in who they are, not who we want them to be. Being a positive early influence to your children and guiding them wisely toward their instinctive purpose is one of the greatest gifts you will ever bestow on them.

Here is what I want you to ask yourself: "What fulfills me? What brings me satisfaction and feelings of success?" Write down in your journal what comes to mind. To help explore your personal fulfillment, finish these sentences:

1) I feel fulfilled when ...
2) I am fulfilled when I've accomplished ...
3) I am fulfilled when I am around ...
4) I am fulfilled when I do ...
5) I am fulfilled when I spend my time ...

For Your Dream, Just Start Somewhere

When I visited Paris, I knew one phrase: *"Je ne parle pas français,"* meaning "I don't speak French." I practiced this phrase over and over for about two hours before I could say it confidently.

I felt terrible not knowing any French, because I had wanted to learn; for twenty years I couldn't wait to get to Paris. Had I learned just one phrase a week for those twenty years, I would have known over a thousand phrases by the time I visited France.

Therefore, what's the lesson? Every week do a little something towards your dream. Leave it as it is—don't judge it, feel guilty, or let other people's expectations about what you need to accomplish throw you off. If you do something each week towards your goal, you'll have, at the very least, fifty-two of something by this time next year.

Henry David Thoreau said, "Go confidently in the direction of your dreams." Just take out your inner compass and walk in that direction. Get one thing done regularly, be that every week or every day, even if it is super simple.

For instance, if you are putting together a cookbook, you can put one recipe in it each week, or even every day. By the time you are done in a year, you will have either 52 or 365 recipes. Both numbers are great!

For myself, I wrote a cooking blog for eleven years. Sometimes, I only included a recipe once a month. Today, I have enough for a full cookbook! When the movie industry puts together an animation film, it sometimes takes a decade or more to go from beginning to screening. All good things take time to complete.

Rest your mind and spirit before you begin on your goal. I used to suffer from goal-and-accomplishment anxiety. Take part of the pressure off by just getting started.

Also, set up your space. Is there a picture you can focus on that inspires or calms you? Something you can look at while you work? Can you keep a relaxing quote nearby? Make sure that it can keep you focused as well as allow you to trust in your own progress.

Remember the old saying, "Slow and steady wins the race"? Set your intention each day of what you would like to accomplish. Would you like to teach yourself a new language by learning a phrase a week? If you want to write, how about writing just one paragraph, and focus only on that today? Maybe you'd like to learn how to cook. Why not just learn how to make one new thing this week? Break your dreams down into small steps and then go confidently in that direction.

My R-Therapy

When I was uncertain about the next steps in my career, I followed what I've come to call my "R-Therapy:" Retreat, Rest, Restore, and Relaunch.

To Retreat might seem like a surprising suggestion, but Retreating is, in my opinion, the most critical part of my R-Therapy. It's essential when you are uncertain or unmotivated—you don't have the energy to accomplish something because you might, in fact, be burnt out. R-therapy is not procrastination; it is a necessary rest to get your creative juices going again. Our body and spirit can only take so much, and we have to be aware of this.

Resting—taking breaks—is essential, and sometimes the only therapy that will put you back on track. I sometimes need to Retreat away from setting goals and having a plan so that I can Rest. It allows me to be in the moment, and do nothing other than focus my energies on being creative: for instance, cooking, painting, or putting a party together.

When I take time away from the pressure of succeeding, I find my inspiration returns and I feel Restored. From there, I can either Re-launch my work in the same direction but with a fresh outlook or take a whole new route with a new idea.

I remember feeling really unmotivated one year—it seemed like I had lost my ability to dream. Of course, this often happens after an exhausting experience, one that can wipe you out and make you feel unenthused about everything.

I knew I had to force myself out of this funk, so I went big and Relaunched the women's conference that I had put on ice for eight years. My purpose for the conference was to encourage other women to live big, and it would seem I needed some of that encouragement, too.

Relaunching my women's conference helped me to immerse myself in those things I found gratifying and helped me to grow. I held my conference for two more years before deciding it was time for me to move on—and in a whole new direction. It was, however, very healing for me, and I'm grateful that my R-Therapy picked me up and put me back into my purpose.

While you may not need to start something like this, just recall a project or hobby that brought you joy and get back to it. Restore your creativity and enthusiasm.

I have always found that to get motivated and feel restored I need to plunge myself in positivity. I watch TED talks. I shop for simple things that will get my senses going, like flowers and beautiful candles. Even if you have to drag yourself out the door to do something you used to love, you need to do it.

Giving back by volunteering in the community is another method, and is always good therapy for the soul. It gets us out of ourselves and into helping others. We've all heard it a million times before: it is better to give than to receive. It's a genuine life law. Everyone feels better when they help others. When you feel uncertain, unmotivated, or burnt out, follow my prescription of R-Therapy: retreat and rest from setting goals for a while so that you can restore yourself and relaunch your dreams once again. It worked for me.

Dreamer Stories I Love

I have always loved reading success stories, particularly about people who've had a hard start in life but persevered, either over other people's opinions of them or just their own perceived limitations. Here are a few dreamer stories that I love.

Walt Disney: The story of Walt Disney is one of perseverance. Fired from a company once upon a time for having a "lack of imagination," Walt's ability to put on his blinders and follow his dream of creating motion movies is one of my favorite stories of a dreamer. He didn't let other people's limited view of his talents take him out of his race.

Ina Garten: Ina once worked for the White House in the Management and Budget Department, but left her prestigious, well-paying position to follow her true passion: opening a catering company and specialty food store called "The Barefoot Contessa." Today, she is the author of countless cookbooks and divides her time between the Hamptons and Paris.

Bal Arneson: This incredible woman "walked away from her unchosen life" and allowed the universe to bring an abundant, authentic life to her. Bal was born in India and moved to Canada to marry an Indian man in an arranged marriage. She eventually fled the marriage and her in-laws for freedom, taking her daughter with her.

Her indomitable spirit built a better life for them both, and she did it by cleaning houses and getting an education to become a teacher. To pay off her school debts, she used her love of cooking healthy Indian food to cater parties. This eventually became the path she followed and, like Ina Garten, she went on to have her own cooking show and write several cookbooks.

Maybe You're Not Certified but You're Probably Qualified

Walt Disney did not have to have an architectural degree to envision Disneyland. Ina Garten and Bal Arneson did not go to culinary school before becoming stars of their own shows and authors of popular cookbooks.

When you've got it, baby, you've got it. And everyone's got something! As soon as a person combines their passion with their talents, they don't need a formal education to prove to be outstanding in their field. Although a formal education is an absolute must in some professions (and sharpening your skills is always recommended), not everyone needs a form of higher learning to be really good at what they do.

Alternatively, not everyone who is certified in their area of practice is exceptional at what they do. Today people can watch an online YouTube tutorial to learn everything from fixing cars to playing guitar. Ina Garten taught herself to cook by reading Martha Stewart cookbooks! As well, my father-in-law Gary and my brother-in-law Jim grew a very successful wireless communications software company back in the 90s with only very little experience in this field. When you do what you love and you work hard at it, when you surround yourself with the best people and have a vision of what you want, the universe will conspire to make things happen.

You might not be certified in the traditional sense, but when you unite your passion with your talents, you'll realize that like Walt, Ina, Bal, Gary, and Jim you are probably well qualified.

Building Your Resumé for Your Big-Picture Dreams

In Chapter Five, I talked about "growing where I was planted." While I worked part-time here and there, for many years I did a lot of work for free so that I could build up my experience and reputation in the field I desired.

For instance, to hone my writing skills, I wrote a monthly column in our local newspaper—for a very small amount of money—just so that I could get the experience. A university asked if they could put one of my articles into a research book in their sports department. My editor told me that if I wanted to, I could charge them. It's not that I didn't think it would be cool to get paid for my article, but at the time, I was just starting out.

I built my resumé doing a lot of other things, too. While I got paid to speak to parents about the Virtues Project, I often did speaking engagements at women's events for free so that I could get my name out there. And it worked! By the time I was ready to give birth to my long-term dream of publishing my first book, I had twelve years of pretty solid experience as a writer and public speaker behind me.

When you are working your way up the ladder towards your dream, it takes time. No experience—whether you get paid for it or not—is ever wasted. Take the courses you need to take, learn as much as you can learn, and get that experience under your belt. Most of all, don't let yourself get thrown off course! Every step towards your dream counts.

Just Book It!

While it's important to look before we leap, sometimes too much thinking can result in procrastination. When you come up with a bright idea or crave to achieve something specific, just book it!

In other words, do something towards your dream that you can't back out of. When I had the idea to put on a women's event in my hometown, I got on the phone and booked the venue before I could talk myself out of it. I generously gave myself a full fourteen months before the day of the event to get organized. To pay for the venue and speakers, I advertised for free in our local paper calling for twenty exhibitors to join me at this first-of-its-kind event in our community.

It was a huge success!

I figured that I'd planned enough warm and successful parties over the years, so this was just going to be on a slightly bigger scale. I looked at the ins and outs in the same way I planned the details of my home parties. I wanted the people who attended my women's conference to feel special: to be inspired and have their senses titillated by delicious food, emotional PowerPoints, uplifting speakers, and stirring music. I called it the Heart & Soul Conference. It was a reflection of both its name and my most extravagant vision to celebrate the women in my community. The effects of this conference are still being felt today.

You, too, will know when you have an idea that comes straight from the heart, because you won't be able to stop thinking about it. It will prove itself an enthusiastic passion.

The Ultimate Two-Step Plan to Success

When I broke down all the steps I'd ever taken to achieve what I desired, it all came down to two steps:

1)   Receive a good idea.
2)   Make it happen.

Anything that comes between those two steps will interrupt the flow.

I remember once allowing insecurity to get in the way of Step Two when people kept asking me why my book wasn't published after working on it for so long. Another time, I worried about not keeping my social media accounts abuzz with daily musings to keep an audience engaged.

The thing is, you don't receive your good ideas from the status quo: you receive them from inspiration. In fact, the very word "inspire," according to the Merriam-Webster dictionary, is derived from Latin and means "to move or guide by divine or supernatural influence."

If you are going to overthink, overthink on the good things; put all of your attention onto your good idea. When you do this, the right stuff will come at the right time. When you get a good idea, just put yourself in the forward-march mindset and eliminate the what-ifs from your thoughts.

Whenever I've come against challenges, I deal with them as they arise. If I fail at something, it's useful—because it's a lesson learned, right? Put all of your energy into your good idea and let yourself be fueled by all that positivity. When it's right, it's right, and you'll know it.

Follow the ultimate two-step plan to success and make it happen! Don't let anything get between those two pivotal steps.

Learn to Cheer Yourself On

Because it took me a long time to write this book, some people began to lose confidence that I would ever get it done. For a long time, they thought I was just talking about my writing, but not actually completing anything.

And while your firefighter might be excited and proud of you, they'll immediately want to know: "Can you make any money at it?" And if you aren't currently making any money at it, "When are you going to start?"

Although this can be a legitimate question (and I know many a fire wife who has experienced this), when they hound us as if it needs to happen *now*, sometimes it can make us feel deterred and unsuccessful. Success in business takes time to build and, if you have a business plan, there will be steps that you will take over time to grow.

One fire wife I know, Rene, is a very successful retail store owner in Fort Langley, British Columbia. Her shop is absolutely gorgeous, and she has now opened in a second location. While her store is popular and she is breaking above even, it will take time for her stores to turn a real profit. However, not only is she passionate about what she does, she has a business plan that will allow her to turn a larger profit in time.

Here's the thing. Your firefighter loves you; and yes, they will pester you about your dream. Firefighters are a controlling bunch, and they may feel that, if they aren't controlling stuff, it will not be well-managed.

Learn ways to keep yourself motivated, but more important-ly, learn how not to absorb other people's projected worry. Building your passion does take time, and you will want to start off small. Go slow, and don't grow too big and too fast before you are ready.

Join networking groups to meet lots of people in your field that can mentor and help you. It's always reassuring to have people in the community to learn from and hear their stories so you don't feel isolated. Get referrals from people you know for great services you'll need, like an instructor, a reputable accoun-tant, a life coach, a designer, and so on.

As well, if you haven't already, learn all you can about the professional side of your passion before you start. So many busi-nesses die because their owners didn't do their due diligence. It's like when people who are home cooks start up a restaurant on a whim, not realizing that 90 percent of restaurants actually fail.

One fire wife I know didn't do her homework before borrowing thousands of dollars for her dream business. Sadly, because of her lack of knowledge and experience, she lost a lot of money and had to file for bankruptcy, which of course affected her whole family.

Be wise, be prepared, and only do what you are passionate about. Do your homework (know what your costs will be, create a marketing plan, know when you will start turning a profit, etc.), and get proper advice from the professionals before going forward.

It's important to show your partner that you are serious about this, but also that you are including them in this dream. It's usually when our other halves don't see the plan in black-and-white that they panic.

After you've done your homework, put your figurative blinders on so that you aren't distracted; keep your eyes on your

201

goal. When it comes to your life's purpose, never settle. Be tireless in pursuing your dreams.

By the Way, Who Cares How Long It Takes?

It's never too late to pursue something that you've always dreamed about, whether your dream is to write a book, travel the world, or start a charity. The reality is that most people cannot simply quit their jobs or stop providing for the people in their lives to pursue their dreams full-time. Just think of the many well-known and famous people who didn't get going until later in life: Julia Child, J.K. Rowling, and Grandma Moses, just to name a few.

On a more personal note, two women I know went back to university to become elementary school teachers after their children got older—a dream both of them had held since they were very young; they graduated in their forties. Some would say my mother is a late bloomer: at the age of seventy-four, after years of working, including at her own small business, she is starting to write. She's written an absolutely hilarious play and a book on seniors' health.

It's been said that we can have it all: just not all at once. The truth is, it's not over until it's over! And though some people may regret not finding their purpose until later in life, I've always believed that whatever years you think you've lost will be made up tenfold in accomplishments stuffed into that shorter period of time. When you have a dream inside you, it wants to get out, no matter how long it takes. Be patient and persevere. It will happen.

Standing Strong in Your Story

I have long admired watching my friend Tara (yes, another Tara) and the story of her life unfold. Today, Tara is happily married to her husband Dean, also a firefighter.

Her post-secondary dreams of going to art school on scholarship ended, however, when she and Dean found out they were expecting their first baby. They were both just eighteen. They were fearful, like most teenagers who find themselves expecting a family while still so young themselves.

With their newborn, Krista, now their first priority, Dean earned money for his young family at a printing press for a large newspaper in Vancouver before becoming a firefighter. Tara turned her gift for art into creating a beautiful home for her family.

Her natural flair for home décor came in handy financially when their family grew with three more kids. She'd refurbish kitchen tables and patio furniture she found on the side of the road. She also made curtains, recovered pillows, and did her own tiling and grouting. Ultimately, Tara embraced her life and grew where she was planted.

Although the odds may have been stacked against Tara and her husband as young parents and eventually a fire couple, her fierce commitment to her family, her unflappable nature, and her quiet resolve came to reap some pretty fantastic rewards.

All people face obstacles throughout their lives, but what sets those of us who rise to the occasion apart from those of us who don't is simply how we deal with the setbacks we are faced with. Where some may see having a family at a very young age as a huge stumbling block from which it would be impossible to recover, to Tara and Dean it was just a life test they passed. It's a great example that adversity will work out for the best, if we just give it our best.

After many years at home with the kids, my friend Tara told us that she had a job interview coming up and was super nervous. If only she could have seen in that moment what the future held for her!

Today, Tara has found her passion as an emergency program officer with the City of Port Coquitlam. She heads a group of 120 crisis volunteers, is second-in-command in her city for emergency preparedness, and now has her own company as a consultant within the corporate sector.

Tara has won city-wide awards for what she does, with many more to come, I'm sure. Additionally, she has just achieved her post-secondary dreams after six years of school to get her Bachelor of Emergency and Security Studies from the Justice Institute of British Columbia.

Everyone, including you, has a story where they refused to give up, resulting in beating the odds and achieving something. It starts with, "they said it wouldn't last" and ends with, "I told you I could do it!" It's a universal story that inspires others to do the same.

These days, Dean and Tara are spending their lives traveling, entertaining family (including grandchildren) at their beautiful second home, a cabin they bought recently, and are going into their third decade of marriage. Though I'm sure there were some tough years when it would have been easier to not push through, it was Tara's wisdom, Dean's sense of humor, and hard work that got them here.

In reflecting upon your life, when did you find yourself at a setback, only to use it as your comeback? Perhaps you found your life in a mess, only to turn it into your message? Many times when we successfully find our life calling, we can use it to give hope to others.

"Standing Strong" Tips From my friend Tara

I emailed my friend Tara recently to get her account of how she went from stay-at-home mom to career woman, and to see if she had any tips and tricks for others. I've really enjoyed reading her advice, but more than that I'm awed at how much her confidence has grown and what she has accomplished. Here's what she has to say.

"Take stock of your unique skillset. For instance, being a stay-at-home mom taught me how to multitask. Being married to a firefighter has taught me great communication skills—you have to know when to be silent or inquisitive based on mood changes and the shift work.

"The skillset that I developed as a housewife and mother transferred seamlessly into my career, and I can assure you that such skills transfer into others as well: planning, gaining social competency, being creative, and practising patience. These lead to a multitude of opportunities, including, if desired, a future career in one of a plethora of industries.

"My confidence has grown in my career. Before, I used to stay quiet when someone did something I disagreed with. Now, I have the confidence to say what I know is right; I know that my opinions matter. I've realized that my decisions are based on years of experience and cultivation. So I can now sit back and say, 'You know what? You can do this; you got this.'

"Make yourself a priority and focus on what is important to you. I surround myself with people who motivate me. I also like to be around others in my profession who have the same passion that I do.

"Plan big and terrific things will happen—but be methodical in your approach. Strategize your projects so that others also see you as a success. Do things that others haven't done, such as apply for grants and awards or produce articles for peer-reviewed journals. Showcase what you do so you can be proud of what you have accomplished. Don't ever be ashamed of this.

"The route I took in life was absolutely unexpected. I was more of a creative person in my youth, and even at a young age I always had a backup plan. I believe you need to be open to all things that come your way. Try to see the bigger picture. Most importantly though, believe in yourself. You can do it!"

My Top Ten Truths for the Dream Journey

I've learned a lot over the years in discovering my dreams. Here are the top ten things I've discovered on my dream journey.

Truth Number 1: When you come up with a dream that is close to your heart, keep it on the down-low for a while. At the beginning of any great idea, you feel rather vulnerable about it, so any negative words will be extremely disheartening. When you do share, make sure it's with a person or persons who are encouraging and trustworthy.

Truth Number 2: Study successful people who have followed their dreams, particularly those who are in an industry you want to work in. Go to lectures to see them, join networking groups to meet them, and attend get-togethers with like-minded people to get motivated. When you study what makes people tick, how they handle adversity, and how they persevere through thick and thin, it will hearten you on your own dream journey.

Truth Number 3: If you don't love it, leave it. Don't stick with something if you've lost the passion. I had a friend who tortured herself to stay in something because she made a commitment to it. Other than your relationship, if you are doing something (whether volunteering, pursuing a career, or attending a club) that you aren't getting anything out of anymore, it's time to explore your options and move on. Don't waste your time; life is too short.

Truth Number 4: Character is destiny. To be successful requires that both you and the people you work closely with have good character. If the people involved in your endeavor don't have good character, they can take you down.

When I volunteered for a charity, we needed to find a local restaurant where we could make soup for women and children fleeing domestic violence. Because time was of the essence, we partnered with a restaurateur whose character we did not know. Wow, what a mistake.

Because the person we were dealing with had no integrity, we paid for it in both stress and food quality. I'd been so passionate about this cause, and sadly I had to leave it because of this person's lack of honor. Fortunately, another venue picked up the cause, and women and children continue to get their soup in our city.

Truth Number 5: You'll meet opposition. It's never been any different. While plenty of people will encourage you along the way, there will be those who make you doubt yourself, your dreams, and everything in between. They might copy you, not credit you, or create drama around you. Know who they are and pay them no mind. But at the same time, be aware they exist.

It has also been said that about 25 percent of the people you meet throughout your life won't like you: maybe for absolutely no reason. It's kind of funny when you think about it, but it's important to recognize it. See it just as a distraction and remember, though it's good to be polite to everyone, don't go on an exhaustive mission trying to convince people of your worth. Be you and stay focused on your dreams.

Truth Number 6: When you do what you love, you'll meet other people who share your values. With them, you will feel naturally energized and loved. It's been said that you are the average of the five people you choose to spend time with. Choose well.

Truth Number 7: You'll meet some obstacles on the path to your dreams, so be prepared at some point on your journey to feel disappointed—maybe even despondent—about your aspirations. In that case, there will come a time when you will be met with a choice: to give up because you don't have the emotional bandwidth to carry on, or to continue because it is still your passion.

If you decide to carry on, and hopefully you do, you will gloriously rise with tougher skin and power enough to cross the finish line. All dreams have hurdles, and some are higher than others. But if you are passionate about the dream in your heart, then you must continue.

Even if you decide to take a break for a while or go on a long vacation to refresh your perspective, then that is what you must do (remember R-Therapy). The only thing that will change after you emerge from your cocoon will be you: resilient, determined, and with an added layer of tenacity.

Truth Number 8: While being of good character will allow you to sleep at night, your good reputation is what others will notice. When people go above and beyond, own up to mistakes and make amends, are honest and hardworking, it gets around.

You can brand yourself, tell everyone how amazing you are, and spend a lot of money promoting yourself, but if you don't have a good reputation, then none of your branding will matter. Aphorism writer Publilius Syrus said (in Latin somewhere between 85 and 43 BCE), "A good reputation is more valuable than money." He was right.

Truth Number 9: Keep your feet on the ground but your head in the clouds. For me, this saying means that we need to balance being an earthy person who is relatable and accepting of others, but who still has a sense of wonder and awe. A sense of wonder about the world and all of its splendor will ignite your creativity. Act like an adult, but keep the heart of a child.

Truth Number 10: When you make achieving your dreams a priority, you'll experience personal satisfaction and joy. All people need to live a life that has meaning; otherwise, they are left with a sense of a life half-lived. Remember, you have a heart that needs to be filled and a bucket list that needs completing.

Unexpected Dreams

Life is what happens to you while you're busy making other plans.
ALLEN SAUNDERS

When I started my journey so many years ago, I never would have thought that this book was what God had planned for me. The idea of becoming a fire wife, let alone writing a book about how to keep a fire relationship strong, was never on my radar. But life has a funny way of delighting us with the unexpected.

Sometimes, our unexpected dreams come from a sense of responsibility or obligation, like fighting for a cause, for others, or for change. Sometimes, we find ourselves going in the opposite direction from what we'd planned.

Like me, some of us go begrudgingly, protesting all the way ... as if settling on a piece of land we didn't want to buy. But then something happens. We wake up feeling that life's going to be okay. Inspiration has arrived, and she's knocking on your door. You realize the land you're on is quite beautiful, and though there's plenty of work to be done, one day you're going to call this place home.

Yes, your dream may be unexpected, but sometimes those are the best ones. It has been for me. Adjustable and flexible: that's what you become. You go from Plan A and hit up Plan B, maybe even C or D. Because sometimes Plan A just means you need *A*nother plan, and plans B, C, and D are just the Best Choice Darling (you'll see).

The universe's options for us are always superior to our own. But before you realize that, you'll experience some life lessons that will change you. They'll be required for your big office with a view. These life lessons are needed to fortify and teach you how to forgive, persevere, and, above all, truly love and believe in yourself.

These days I have a level of joy in my marriage, my life, and my dreams that I could not have comprehended in my early days. Philosopher and theologian Søren Kierkegaard famously said, "Life can only be understood backwards; but it must be lived forwards."

From the wisdom my friend Joanne gave me to "hold on" in my marriage, to the pledge I made to write a book that *ironically kept me committed to my marriage*, I have learned that Søren Kierkegaard was right. And in looking back over my life now, it all makes perfect sense.

It will for you, too. Just be open to wise advice from decent people, listen to your instincts, and trust that those rough patches will smooth over in time because of it.

This year is my husband's and my twenty-fifth anniversary. It's also the year I give birth to my book. The perfect timing of its release has proven to be symbolic. Who knew? There is an old Yiddish proverb that says, "When we plan, God laughs." I guess it was kind of amusing, thinking I had it all figured out.

Though we're now at the end of this book, the reality is you're just getting started. For you, a new chapter—a new season—is about to begin. But here's what I need you to remember as you forge ahead on the path of your relationships, your big life, and your dreams. You've got this. You are powerful. You are influential. You are invaluable.

You're also an inspiration. If I could get to this great place in my life and relationship, then you can, too. I want you to stand strong. Stay courageously committed to yourself, your growth, and to your *amour propre* because you're worth it.

And guess what? It's going to turn out better than you imagined. Until then, my friend, you can smile at your future.

XOXO

Tara McIntosh

Permissions

Ollivier, Debra. *What French Women Know: About Love, Sex, and Other Matters of the Heart and Mind.* The Penguin Group (Canada), 2009.

Templeton, John. *Worldwide Laws of Life: 200 Eternal Spiritual Principles.* Templeton Foundation, Inc. Templeton Press, 1997.

Acknowledgments

I can't tell you how excited I am to finally be at the acknowledgements part of writing this book. After several great years of writing, I finally get to reflect on the special people in my life and what this journey has meant to me.

First and foremost, I give thanks to the big guy in the sky, my God, for directing my steps, answering my prayers, and not answering my prayers sometimes, too. His ways are always best, and I am grateful for the life he has blessed me with.

Thank you to all of my firefighter friends! I've enjoyed so many super conversations with you around many tables, and you've given me incredible insight into how you feel. Considering there was significant suspicion at first surrounding this book and what it might entail, I'm happy you've all come to realize it was a positive book for you too!

What I came to learn through years of hanging out with you guys is that you are a very vulnerable group who needs their family. I admire and honor all of you, and thank you profusely for protecting our communities and giving us true heroes to look up to.

I am also beholden to my gorgeous fire wife friends who likewise joined me at the table (over champagne, of course) and validated that what I was experiencing with my firefighter was, indeed, universal. You girls are the best! Thank you to Tara Stroup, Leanne Dean, Kathleen Nadalin, Simone Davidson, and my friend Sheila Alwell (our friendship is true happenstance, my soup sista). These fire wives are the epitome of what standing strong in your relationship, life, and dreams looks like, and they have my admiration.

I also want to thank those fire wives whom I interviewed, but didn't want to be mentioned by name in this book. Understandably, our stories are very personal, and I appreciate you all.

What would I ever do without my beautiful friends and family? I have relied on your talent, counsel, and endless assistance for any new project I have ever undertaken. And, of course, for making my world a much sweeter place.

From my women's conference, to politics, to making soup for women and children in need, I will forever be thankful to my long-time supporters: my friends who are family and my family who are friends. You all came together to make our community a more caring place for others. I love and adore all of you.

Now, to the most important people in my life ... my husband Tom. I love you more than life, hon! From Kelowna and Leavenworth to Paris, London, and Croatia, there is no one else I'd rather enjoy life's adventures with. You've been my rock and the greatest father to our children. We seriously complement one another, and I thank you for your honesty, integrity, and humor. I love you, hon. Now, get outta here!

Thank you to my greatest gifts, our sons, Brayden and Liam. My world only got better with you two in it, and it's been my privilege to have raised such great men. You two reside in the deepest part of my heart, and have been my greatest teachers. To say I love you both so much is an understatement.

Thank you to my mom and best friend Valerie, who has consistently been my biggest cheerleader since I was little. You always made me feel as though I was better than I actually was.

If my husband has been my rock, then you have been the wind beneath my wings. We have taken this creative journey together, Mom, and I thank you for always being there. I am excited for what your future holds with your own great writings. I love you, Mom!

Thank you to my sister Keeli, who really encouraged me to make this book my priority. Since we were young, I always felt like the two of us were twins. Our deep bond has always been a special one. I have always felt so lucky to have had both a sister and a best friend all in one. I love you.

Thank you to my incredible and wise-beyond-their-years niece and nephew, Kora and Jake. It has been a pleasure being your Tante, and I have loved watching you grow. I can't wait to see what this beautiful world has in store for you; but, more importantly, what great things you have in store for the world. I love you two so much!

To my Dad. I really wish that my Daddio, Richard William Knowles, were here on earth to finally see my book published. He bought me my first briefcase and introduced me to *Meet the Press* and *The New York Times*. I miss our conversations over coffee, but know that he was always a very proud Dad and Grandpa—and still is, I'm sure!

I must also acknowledge my Grandma, B. Elizabeth, also known as Bootsy. This beautiful woman of faith taught me so much, and fed me well to boot. I loved our deep conversations, and I always think of her when I read Psalm 23. Wishing I could still pick up that phone and call her.

I am also grateful to my husband's parents, my in-laws Donna and Gary McIntosh whose partnership, values and extreme generosity not only gave me my husband Tom, but the abundant life I dreamt about from the time I was a little girl.

I want to thank my beautiful friend, Tammy Lewis, whose heart is as warm as the summer sun. My friend, you speak words that lift me so high and make me feel so loved. You are a true soul sister, and I am grateful for our friendship.

I would also like to thank my friend Shirley Weir, who has encouraged me from the moment we met. She is living proof that having a vision and working towards your goals equals a dream come true!

Last, but certainly not least, I would like to thank both Nina Shoroplova and Michelle Balfour for editing and organizing this book. Both women have been so positive and encouraging while guiding me honestly, but thoughtfully, through this process. I am so very glad it was you two. I feel very lucky and very grateful to you both. Thank you.

Author Bio

Tara McIntosh lives in Port Moody, British Columbia, with the loves of her life—her firefighter husband Tom, their two sons, Brayden and Liam, and their dog Bentley. In her free time, she entertains friends and family, cooks, writes, and contributes to making positive changes in her community through speaking, organizing events, standing for justice, encouraging others, and hopefully making the world a better place.

Connect With Tara McIntosh on Social Media:
 Facebook @firewifewise
 Instagram @firewifewise
 Twitter @firewifewise

Or on Her Website: www.firewifewise.com

APPENDIX

Useful Resources

Books

Angelou, Maya. *The Collected Autobiographies of Maya Angelou.* Modern Library, 2004.

Allen, Jimmy. *Extreme Heat: A Firefighter's Life.* Manor House Publishing Inc., 2007.

Brown, Brene. *Rising Strong.* Spiegel & Grau, 2017.

Bryne, Rhonda. *The Secret.* Atria Books, Beyond Words Publishing, 2006.

Cameron, Julia. *The Artist's Way: A Spiritual Path To Higher Creativity.* Tarcher/Perigree, 1992.

Carlson, Richard. *Don't Sweat the Small Stuff ... and it's all Small Stuff.* Hachette Books, 1997.

Cohen, Alan. *Dare to Be Yourself: How to Quit Being an Extra in Other People's Movies and Become the Star of Your Own.* Reprint Ed., Ballantine Books, 1994.

Gladwell, Malcolm. *Outliers: The Story of Success.* Little, Brown and Company, 2008.

Gray, John. *Men are from Mars, Women are from Venus.* Harper Collins, 1992.

Farrel, Bill and Pam Farrel. *Men Are Like Waffles, Women Are Like Spaghetti: Understanding and Delighting in Your Differences.* Harvest House, 2001.

Hay, Louise. *You Can Heal Your Life.* Hay House Inc.; 10th Ed. 1984

Huffington, Arianna. *The Sleep Revolution: Transforming Your Life, One Night at a Time.* Harmony, 2017.

Jonekos, Staness and Wendy Klein, MD. *The Menopause Makeover: The Ultimate Guide to Taking Control of Your Health and Beauty During Menopause.* Harlequin, 2010.

Kiyosaki, Robert and Sharon Lechter. *Rich Dad, Poor Dad.* Warner Books, 2000.

McGraw, Phil. *The Life Code: The New Rules for Winning in the Real World.* Bird Street Books, 2013.

Morrow Lindbergh, Anne. *Gift from the Sea: 50th Anniversary Edition.* Second Ed. Pantheon, 1991.

Mundy, Jon, PhD. *Living A Course in Miracles: An Essential Guide to the Classic Text.* Sterling Ethos, 2011

Northrup, Christiane, MD. *Women's Bodies, Women's Wisdom: Creating Physical and Emotional Health and Healing.* Revised Ed. Bantam, 2010.

Northrup, Christiane, MD. *The Wisdom of Menopause: Creating Physical and Emotional Health During the Change.* Revised Ed. Bantam, 2012.

Ollivier, Debra. *What French Women Know: About Love, Sex, and Other Matters of the Heart and Mind.* The Penguin Group (Canada), 2009.

Oz, Mehmet, MD and Michael Roizen, MD. *YOU: The Owners Manual: An Insider's Guide to the Body that Will Make You Healthier and Younger.* William Morrow Paperbacks, 2013.

Peale, Norman Vincent. *The Power of Positive Thinking.* Simon & Schuster, 1952.

Richardson, Cheryl. *Take Time for Your Life: A 7-Step Program for Creating the Life You Want.* Broadway Books, 1998.

Somers, Suzanne. *I'm Too Young for This! The Natural Hormone Solution to Enjoy Perimenopause.* Harmony, 2013

Tieger, Paul D. and Barbara Barron-Tieger. *Do What You Are: Discover the Perfect Career for You Through the Secrets of Personality Type.* Little, Brown and Company, 1992.

Tieger, Paul D. and Barbara Barron-Tieger. *Nurture by Nature: Understand Your Child's Personality Type—And Become a Better Parent.* Little, Brown and Company, 1997.

Zukav, Gary. *The Seat of the Soul.* Simon & Schuster, 1989.

Magazines

Delicious. 2003 – present. London: England

Olive. 2003 – present. London: England

Oprah. 2000 – present. New York City: USA

Martha Stewart Living. 1990 – present. Des Moines: USA

Psychology Today. 1967 – present. New York: USA.

Success. 1897 – present. Dallas: USA

Unearth Women. 2018 – present. New York: USA

Where Women Create. 2009 – present. Oshawa: Canada

Websites

dnaPower: www.dnapower.com

Hayhouse Radio: www.hayhouseradio.com

Hyperthyroid Mom: www.hypothyroidmom.com

Menopause Chicks Cracking Open the Conversation: www.menopausechicks.com

Oz: www.doctoroz.com

SARK: www.planetsark.com

Spiritual Cinema Circle: www.spiritualcinemacircle.com

The Myers Way: www.amymyersmd.com

The Virtues Project: www.virtuesproject.com

Firefighter and Fire Wife Resources for Trauma, PTSD, Leadership, Family Life, and Health

Fire Engineering: www.fireengineering.com

Firefighter Wife: www.firefighterwife.com

Fire House: www.firehouse.com

Fire Rescue: www.firerescuemagazine.com

PTSD Association of Canada: http://www.ptsdassociation.com

The Lifeline Canada Foundation: https://thelifelinecanada.ca

Influential Mentors

Helen Burns of Relate Church in Surrey BC inspired Chapter Eight, You Are Gifted and Celebrate Your Future. From In-To-Me-See (Intimacy) to honing your gifts, her words have cemented into my brain and have become a large part of my language. Now you get to hear her influence and wisdom.

Glynis Sherwood of Glynis Sherwood Counselling inspired parts of Chapter Six. I've mentioned my counselor many times throughout this book. From going low contact, chakra work, and setting boundaries, Glynis' counseling has been beyond helpful.

Recipes

How to Stretch a Roast Chicken

My friend Sheila grew up in Ireland as one of four children. Her mother, being a widow, had to watch her pennies, and taught her daughter the importance of stretching a roast chicken into several meals: from soup and sandwiches, to chicken pot pie and chicken salad. What a great lesson in cooking and budgeting. Here are some ways I stretch a 3 – 5 pound roast chicken after the first meal:

Chicken Stir Fry

2 Tbsp. Oil
½ Cup Onion, diced
2 Cloves Garlic, chopped
1 Cup Mushrooms, sliced
1 Cup Red, Yellow, or Green Pepper, sliced
1 Cup Chopped Broccoli
½ Cup Canned Water Chestnuts, drained (optional)
¼ Cup Peanuts (optional)
1-2 Cups Cooked Chicken, cubed

Stir Fry Sauce
½ Cup Chicken Broth
¼ Cup Soy Sauce

1 Tbsp. Ginger, shredded
1 Tbsp. Five-Spice
1 Tbsp. Cornstarch

Put oil into medium-sized frying pan over medium heat. Add onion, garlic, mushrooms, pepper, and broccoli. Sauté until tender.

Add water chestnuts and peanuts (optional). Add cooked chicken.

For sauce, stir together ingredients. Mix well, ensuring there are no little lumps. Pour into the pan over chicken and vegetables. Stir and allow to reduce for approximately 10 minutes. Sauce will thicken.

Serve over your favorite rice. Serves 4-6 people

Chinese Chicken Salad

454 g. Box Fettuccine Noodles (approx. 4 cups dry pasta or 1lb. cooked)
2 Tbsp. Sesame Oil
1-2 Cups Cooked Chicken, cubed or shredded
2 Carrots, peeled and shredded
4 Green Onions, sliced
2 Red Peppers, chopped
2 Yellow Peppers, chopped
1 Cup Mushrooms, sliced
½ Cup Peanuts, chopped
¼ Cup Chow Mein noodles
¼ Cup Cilantro Leaves (optional)

Dressing
1 Large Garlic Clove, minced
4 Tbsp. Soya Sauce

⅛ Cup Olive Oil
2 Tbsp. Brown Sugar
1 Tbsp. Hot Sauce (optional)

Bring a medium-sized pot of water to a boil and add 2 tbsp. of salt. Then add package of fettuccine noodles. Cook until *al dente* (about 8-10 minutes). Drain pasta in a colander. Put into medium-sized serving bowl and add sesame oil so pasta doesn't stick.

Once pasta is cool, toss with chicken, vegetables, and peanuts.

In a separate bowl, mix together the dressing. Pour over noodle salad, toss, and top with ¼ cup chow mien noodles and ¼ cup cilantro leaves (optional).

Easy Chicken Wellington

For this recipe, I like to buy puff pastry that has already been rolled out, but if you can't find that, simply defrost the puff pastry and put a little flour on a workspace to roll out.

1 Package Store-Bought Puff Pastry.
4 Tbsp. Butter
½ Onion, chopped
½ Cup Leeks, chopped
2 Cups Spinach
1 Cup Mushrooms, chopped
1-2 Cups Chicken, shredded
1 tsp. Thyme
1 tsp. Rosemary
Pinch Salt
Pinch Pepper
Egg Wash

2 Egg Yolks
2 Tbsp. Milk

Divide pastry into two. Once both sheets have been rolled out into rectangles, place one sheet onto an ungreased cookie sheet. Set aside.

In a pan over medium heat, add butter and sauté vegetables. Sauté until vegetables are soft and liquid evaporates. Add shredded chicken and stir. Add your favorite seasonings such as thyme or rosemary as well as a pinch of both salt and pepper.

Evenly distribute chicken mixture over puff pastry on the cookie sheet, leaving a 1 inch border all around the edges. Top with the second half of puff pastry and, using a fork, seal along the edges.

Brush puff pastry with egg wash. Bake according to pastry package instructions.

Favorite Recipes

Below are some of my favorite recipes for quick and delicious meals.

Red Wine Sausages over Buttery Mashed Potatoes

8-10 Large British or Bratwurst Sausages
2 Tbsp. Butter
1 Onion, diced
1 Cup Mushrooms, sliced
2 Tbsp. Flour
1 Cup Beef Broth
½ Cup Red Wine
1 Tsp. Garlic Powder (or fresh or roasted, if you prefer)
Salt and pepper

Bake sausages at 350 degrees for 20 minutes and set aside.

In a large saucepan over medium heat, melt butter. Add onions and mushrooms and cook until soft. Add flour and whisk. Then add the red wine and beef broth; continue whisking so lumps don't form. Bring to a soft boil and reduce the liquid by half. Add seasonings.

Turn the heat down to low and add the cooked sausages. Spoon sauce over the sausages and let simmer for about 10 minutes.

Serve sausages over mashed potatoes and pour juices over top.

My Easy Mashed Potatoes

I've learned a couple of things about making mashed potatoes. Don't over-boil them, don't let them sit in the water, and use a really good potato masher. I actually like to use two potato mashers: the traditional wavy one to break up the potatoes, and then one that has small holes like a ricer to get out the lumps.

6 Medium-Sized Yukon Gold Potatoes
1 Tbsp. Garlic Powder (fresh or roasted if you prefer)
½ Cup Butter
¼ Cup Milk, Cream, or Chicken Broth

Boil sliced potatoes for 20 minutes or until tender. Once done, drain using a colander and allow to rest for about 2 minutes.

Put potatoes back into the pot, add butter and seasonings, and mash. Add liquid and allow to sit for about a minute before continuing to mash until smooth.

Grandma Bootsy's Chicken and Dumpling Soup

I usually make a chicken-and-dumpling soup from either a couple of leftover rotisserie chickens or a homemade roast chicken. The dumplings, which are both fluffy and dense, are the star in this recipe. Choose and sauté your favorite vegetables, add some broth, and voila: a cozy dinner that should stretch for 2 meals.

The Chicken Soup

2 Tbsp. Olive or Vegetable Oil
2 Medium-sized Carrots, peeled and chopped
1 Large Onion, peeled and diced
4 Celery Stalks, chopped
2 Cloves Garlic, minced (or ½ tbsp. garlic powder)
2-3 Cups Cooked Chicken, chopped
6-8 Cups Chicken Broth
1 Can Diced Tomatoes (optional)
Salt and Pepper
Favorite Spices (I like 1 tsp. thyme and 1 tsp. rosemary, or 1 tbsp. fresh tarragon)

The Dumplings
2 Cups All-Purpose Flour
4 Tsp. Baking Powder
1 Tsp. Salt
¼ Tsp. Pepper
1 Large Egg
2 Tbsp. Melted Butter
¾-1 Cup Milk
2 Tbsp. each of your favorite herb or spice

In a medium-sized pot, heat oil and add carrots, sautéing until almost soft. Next add the celery and onions, continuing to stir. When the onions and celery are soft, add garlic and stir for a minute.

Next add the chicken, broth, and 1 tin of canned tomatoes (optional) to the pot and bring to a boil. If the soup becomes too thick, simply add more water or possibly more chicken broth for flavour.

Be ready with the dumpling dough. Make sure you have a lid handy.

Method for Dumplings

Blend the first four ingredients, and then add egg, butter, and ¾ cup of milk. If the mixture seems too dry, you can add up to another ¼ cup of milk. Mix well. Once it's mixed, add your herbs and spices. I like to add 1 Tbsp. of chopped parsley leaves and a tablespoon of smoked paprika.

Once the soup is boiling, add the dumpling dough 1 heaping tablespoon at a time. Turn the heat down to low. Finally, put the lid on the soup pot and keep it closed for at least 20 minutes to allow the dumplings to fluff up. No peeking! To test the dumplings, take one out of the pot and slice it in half to see if it is cooked to your liking. They should be tender. Turn off the heat and serve.

Lemon-Scented Italian Braid Cookies

From my neighbourhood to yours, please enjoy my favorite childhood Italian braid cookies.

3 Eggs
½ Cup Sugar
½ Cup Oil
2 Lemons (the juice of two lemons and the zest from one lemon)
1 Tbsp. Almond Extract (or white vanilla extract)
3 Cups Flour
3 Tsp. Baking Powder

In one bowl, mix together the eggs, sugar, and oil. Juice both lemons and take the zest from one. Add almond extract and set aside.

Mix the flour and the baking powder together and then add to the liquid ingredients, mixing until they form a nice dough.

To make the cookie braids, measure out a scoop of cookie dough until you have 12 scoops. Then roll each one out on floured surface to make a rope. Make an upside-down "U" with the cookie dough rope, bringing the right side over the left side. Wrap it under and back to the front. Repeat until a cookie braid is completed. Seal the end so that it holds together, and then put them on a greased cookie sheet.

Bake at 350 degrees for 15 minutes.

Other Books
By Tara McIntosh

Let's stay connected! Come and join our community
at www.firewifewise.com
for articles on Fire Life, starting a Fire Wife book club,
for recipes and more!

CPSIA information can be obtained
at www.ICGtesting.com
Printed in the USA
LVHW010916060521
686676LV00002B/121